Unsearchable Riches

Unsearchable Riches

Selected Sermons
by
Rev Donald MacLean

REFORMATION PRESS

British Library Cataloguing in Publication Data

ISBN 978-1-872556-06-2

© Reformation Press 2013

PUBLISHED BY

Reformation Press, 11 Churchill Drive, Stornoway
Isle of Lewis, Scotland HS1 2NP

www.reformationpress.co.uk

FIRST PAPERBACK EDITION
May 2013

FIRST HARDBACK EDITION
ISBN 978-1-872556-07-9
May 2013

FIRST KINDLE EDITION
ISBN 978-1-872556-08-6
May 2013

TYPESET BY

Melvaig Typesetting

PRINTED BY
www.lulu.com

Contents

Foreword

Reformation Press is pleased to make available this collection of sermons by Rev Donald MacLean. Mr MacLean (1915–2010) was a pre-eminent minister of the Free Presbyterian Church of Scotland. Ordained in 1948, he continued preaching for over sixty years, including after his retirement from the ministry in 2000 until a few months before his death. Many thousands heard his powerful preaching throughout these years and under the blessing of the Holy Spirit this was profitable to many, both in his own Church and far beyond.

The present volume contains twelve sermons taken from various times in his long ministry. They are a small selection of sermons which were recommended by some of his hearers as particularly special or memorable. Most of these sermons were preached at ordinary Lord's Day services in his own congregation. The typical length of a sermon was around sixty minutes and Mr Maclean preached a minimum of three sermons every week—two on the Lord's Day and one at the midweek prayer meeting. Generally he preached from a different text every time, yet every sermon is a thoughtfully structured exposition of the text and contains something fresh and helpful to the hearers. Mr MacLean's sermons are characterised by clear and plain teaching, prioritising directness over spiritualisations and extravagant rhetorical flourishes.

The sermons preached in the Glasgow congregation were regularly recorded throughout Mr Maclean's forty-year pastorate there. These recordings are a rich resource and audio CDs or MP3 files are available from the Free Presbyterian Bookroom (133 Woodlands Road, Glasgow, G3 6LE). A small number of recordings are also available online (www.fpchurch.org.uk).

In preparing the selected sermons for publication the first step was to make a verbatim transcription of the recording. This transcription was then edited in order to make the content suitable for reading, keeping as close as possible to the original wording while making whatever concessions were necessary for the sake of the reader. This principally consisted of light editing of grammar and correction of ambiguities and verbal slips, together with minor reworking of text for conciseness or clarity.

Mr MacLean approved of this project to publish his sermons. Although he sadly passed away at an early stage of the transcription and editing process, he read and approved of the editing of one of the sermons (Sermon 7, on 1 Kings 19:11-12), and the remaining nine sermons were edited on the same principles.

The twelve sermons included in this volume cover a variety of subjects, including the glory of the gospel, the necessity of personal religion, and Christ's mediatorial work as Prophet, Priest and King. This volume also includes a sample of Mr MacLean's Communion sermons, both a preparatory service and an 'action sermon' (preached prior to the administration of the Lord's Supper on the Communion Sabbath). The volume ends with the final sermon Mr MacLean preached, in Inverness in 2009.

A number of conventions have been adopted in this volume. Some but not all of the many scriptural quotations and allusions are referenced in parentheses, and when verses were quoted with minor alterations to fit the context, these have been retained where appropriate rather than giving the exact quotation from the Authorised Version. In quotations from the Scottish Metrical Psalms, line breaks are denoted by a slash mark (/).

The publisher would like to acknowledge with gratitude the help of many individuals during the production of this volume. Many people kindly suggested sermons which were suitable for publication. Meticulous tran-scription was undertaken by Flora Campbell, Fiona Campbell, Catherine Dickie, Johan Dickie, Ruth Jardine and Mary Ramsay. Rev David Campbell and Catherine Dickie ably assisted with editing. Alex MacAskill provided professional expertise in layout and cover design. Thanks are also due to James Dickie for preparing the cover photograph and enhancing the scanned photograph of Mr MacLean. Finally, the publisher wishes to record his gratitude to Murdo MacLean, Mr MacLean's younger son, for his encouragement to proceed with this project and for permission to use a professional photograph of his father. Murdo also rendered invaluable assistance to David Campbell in providing details for the biographical sketch.

It is planned that further volumes of Mr MacLean's sermons will be issued, God willing. Suggestions of sermons for inclusion in further volumes will be warmly welcomed—please send an email to:- orders@reformationpress.co.uk. In issuing this first volume of the series, the publisher echoes the petition with which Mr MacLean concluded many sermons: 'May the Lord bless his Word.'

THE PUBLISHER
Stornoway
April 2013

Biographical sketch
of Rev Donald MacLean

Donald MacLean was born in Glasgow on 3rd June 1915. His father, also Donald, was from Coigach, Wester Ross, and his mother, Rachel MacLeod, was born on the Isle of Raasay. He was the eldest of four children, with two sisters and a brother who died in infancy. The family moved to the Shawlands district of Glasgow in his early youth. Donald MacLean was brought up in the Free Presbyterian Church and he adhered steadfastly to this stand for Reformed orthodoxy throughout his life. This brief biographical sketch will look at some of the influences which shaped his preaching and will offer an appreciation of his preaching.

Early influences

Among the early influences which shaped his character was the preaching of godly and earnest ministers. Donald MacLean was brought up under the ministry of Rev Neil Cameron until his mid teenage years and walked to the place of worship up to four miles each Sabbath. His memory of Mr Cameron's preaching was limited but one feature which he did recall was the solemn warnings which Mr Cameron gave concerning the revivalism of Moody and Sankey, which he rightly viewed as having done huge damage to the Scottish churches. From the death of Mr Cameron in 1932 until he joined the war effort in 1941 Donald MacLean was under the ministry of Rev Roderick Mackenzie. He held both these ministers in high esteem and their approach to preaching was no doubt to some extent replicated in his own preaching style.

Until a fuller biography is written, little can be said of Donald MacLean's boyhood years. He was educated at the Albert Road Academy in Pollokshields and after completing his schooling he worked for Walter and WB Galbraith, a firm of chartered accountants. He began his training within the firm in 1933 and qualified as a chartered accountant in 1939. He had prospects of becoming a partner in the firm after the war, but divine providence had other paths for him to walk. It was in this period that he came under the power of the truth which led eventually to his making a profession of his faith in Christ in 1937. The influence of one close friend—William MacLean—was central to his being first awakened. This friend acknowledged that he himself had been converted and this fact raised the solemn questions in Donald MacLean's conscience as to his own spiritual condition.

Saving change and call to the ministry

Donald MacLean did not experience a true spiritual appreciation of the gospel until his twenties. The danger of delay in seeking salvation was something which he often stressed in the pulpit. The war years, in which so many young men died, further impressed on his mind the importance of young people seeking Christ early, thus preparing him to sound that note in his preaching with real personal sympathy.

An informative obituary written for the Free Presbyterian Magazine (October 2010) gives the details of the great spiritual change through which Donald MacLean passed. This account is all the more profitable in that it is reproduced largely in his own words. His struggles under a sense of sin and finding peace for his soul were not greatly prolonged. He obtained a great sense of gospel liberty and assurance in November of 1935, but records that he was still troubled that he could not find his experience being addressed in the preaching. It was over the next number of months that he found and made much use of the sermons of Rev Jonathan Rankin Anderson, who had ministered at Knox's Tabernacle in Glasgow in the 19th century and whose congregation later joined the Free Presbyterian Church. In a memoir of Isabella and Barbara Morton, two godly women in the Glasgow congregation, reference is made to the attachment which these two women had for the sermons of Mr Anderson and how they encouraged others to read them. Mr MacLean identified these two women as having a considerable influence on him in the early years of his Christian course (and later provided the introduction to their memoir). This common interest in the sermons and ministry of Mr Anderson was doubtless a formative influence on Mr MacLean.

Donald MacLean's war service began in March 1941. Interestingly, he felt guided by the Word of God to the choice of serving in the Royal Navy and also felt some assurance upon entering that service that he would be preserved through the great conflict. The passage which he felt spoke to his case in this regard was Psalm 68:22: 'The Lord said, I will bring again from Bashan, I will bring my people again from the depths of the sea.' He served for the remaining years of the conflict with the Royal Navy and attained the rank of lieutenant. He spent some time in West Africa and in the United Kingdom, training officers in the art of hunting U-boats. Many have heard of his experiences during the war years and he frequently referred to them in old age. What came out of these accounts was a sense that he was willing to stand alone for his principles and convictions and that he obtained the respect of many around him for doing so, even when it cost him in other ways.

Mr MacLean's war service in the Royal Navy ended in January 1946. His circumstances in life made it very likely that he would be employed for further service and he anticipated being required to go to the Far East after the war. This was not to be, however. In his own account of his call to the ministry he records that he had given much thought to what he ought to do after the war and the idea of returning to his former employment filled him with dread. While he had considered the ministry during these years he did not then have the needed light to enter upon it. His desires for that work however could not be put aside and events in providence eventually closed him in to his duty.

In his own account of these events he recalled being present at a communion season in North Tolsta (presumably in March 1945), where the prayer and discourse of Rev Malcolm Gillies (the minister over the then joint Stornoway and Tolsta congregation) were of great help to him in directing him towards the ministry of the gospel. Two particular portions of Scripture were also confirmatory at this time. In opening the question meeting at the communion in Stornoway in August 1945 Mr Gillies spoke with great directness on the work of the ministry from Titus 2:14. Again in private Mr MacLean found much needed direction from Jeremiah 15:19: 'And if thou take forth the precious from the vile, thou shalt be as my mouth.' Other portions of truth were also helpful to him. On 24th September 1945 he appeared before his kirk session in Glasgow to be accepted as a divinity student. Unusually for Mr MacLean, he recalls breaking down in tears a number of times during and after the session meeting from a sense of the Lord's goodness. He had been informed also on entering the session that Mr Gillies had passed away earlier that day.

Entering the ministry

Following the procedures of presbyterian church government, the recommendation of the Glasgow kirk session was sent to the presbytery. The Southern Presbytery duly received Mr MacLean as a divinity student and he was placed under the care of the Training of the Ministry Committee. From January 1946 and through the summer months of that year he pursued his university studies. The convener of the Committee informed the Synod in May 1946 that 'Mr Donald MacLean's good progress in Hebrew and Greek at Glasgow University will enable him (DV) to begin divinity classes in November.' There were in total six students of the Church at this time, with several of these preparing to enter mission work at home and overseas. Mr MacLean and his life-long friend William MacLean began their divinity training in November 1946 under Rev Donald A. Macfarlane in Dingwall. At the Synod of the following year (1947) it was agreed that the time spent studying Hebrew and Greek at University were to be taken as equivalent to a year of divinity training and that the year in Dingwall was counted as their second year. The two friends then went to study under Rev Donald Beaton in Oban who recorded in his report to the Synod in the following year that they were both 'of more than average ability,' making the duty of teaching them a pleasure to him.

On 22nd December 1948 Donald MacLean was ordained to the office of the ministry and inducted to the charge of the congregation at Portree on the Isle of Skye. The call was signed by 303 persons. His pastorate in Portree continued until June 1960. During that time he married Grace Macqueen, from Inverness, who was his beloved companion for 53 years. She steadfastly gave her husband much practical support throughout his ministry, particularly in visiting the sick and housebound and in entertaining guests. They had four children—two sons and two daughters.

Mr MacLean's interest in young people was evident throughout his ministry, and his editorship of the Young People's Magazine during this period in Skye reflected that in its pages each month. One of his earlier hearers in Portree recalls of his preaching at this time that its effect on a young person was 'that you couldn't be at the vanities of the world on Saturday and sit comfortably in the pew on Sabbath—the preaching forced you to choose between the two.' Not only is this a testimony to the work of the Holy Spirit in conviction of sin (which affects in a measure everyone brought out of Satan's kingdom), but it reflects a conspicuous feature of Mr MacLean's preaching, namely that he did not shun to declare the terrors of the law along with the riches of the gospel. The absence of this faithfulness in preachers was to him a sign that the Lord had not called them to that office.

Mr MacLean was an active and earnest pastor and the anecdote has survived that he made it his habit each Monday morning to make personal visits to those of his congregation who had failed to attend the services the previous day. This was partly how he built up the congregational attendance at church services. Several were converted under his ministry. He made the following personal reflection concerning his ministry in Portree: 'Although there was this outward gathering, and more attention to the Word of God, yet there was no real progress by way of public profession. I felt this to be quite a trial, when I knew there were some there to whom the gospel had been made precious. It was a feature of the beginning of my ministry, that most of the people who were converted under my preaching had this experience at communion seasons being held in other congregations. It seemed a strange providence, but it would only be proper for me to say with the Divine Redeemer, "Even so, Father; for so it seemed good in thy sight."'

His stance in defence of the Lord's Day was conspicuous in Skye and he became a known voice on several moral issues, including the relaxation of local licensing laws and the sins of worldliness among professing Christians. Unsparing in his pulpit warnings, he regularly alluded in his sermons to political as well as local events about which he saw it expedient to warn people. He also followed the previously mentioned example of Rev Neil Cameron, by warning both in the pulpit and in the press against the Billy Graham campaigns of the 1950s and the Luis Palau campaigns in the 1980s.

Ministry in Glasgow and the wider church

After twelve years in the Isle of Skye, Donald MacLean accepted a call from the congregation of St Jude's, Glasgow, the same congregation in which he had been brought up. His pastorate there began on 14th June 1960 and continued until his retirement on 29th February 2000. For these forty years he laboured faithfully in preaching, pastoring and ruling within the Church of Christ. The duties entrusted to him by Synod of his Church are carefully enumerated in a comprehensive Synod tribute to his memory (May 2011). One feature of his tenure in positions of trust and responsibility high-lighted in this account is that he was prepared to bring his term of service to Church committees and courts to an end when he saw the time was right for doing so. He made it known that his primary reason for doing this was to enable him to continue to give his focus to preaching.

Mr MacLean first visited the Church's Mission in what is now Zimbabwe in 1955 and again in 1965. His hearty interest in the African mission of the Church was not sentimental but grew out of a deep love for souls and a desire to see the gospel being spread among all nations. It also arose from a respect for the remarkable providence of God which led to the formation and preservation of the Mission in its earlier days, to which he often referred. (Details of the establishment of the African Mission can be found in several publications, including *John Boyana Radasi,* by Jean Nicolson.) It was a matter of great concern to Mr MacLean to secure and build on the link between Scotland and Rhodesia which Rev Neil Cameron had so diligently forged. In his role as Clerk of the Foreign Missions Committee, he showed a zealous care that foreign missions be established on a scriptural footing. Mr MacLean believed that there ought to be a clear distinction between the responsibility of the Church of Christ to obey the Saviour's commission to preach the gospel to every creature and the auxiliary services such as schools and hospitals which have sometimes come to represent missionary endeavours today. He saw that the duty of preachers to declare the unsearchable riches of Christ forbade them from becoming entangled in 'the affairs of this life' which do not belong to the Church of Christ as such.

Another significant way in which Mr MacLean served the Church was as the tutor of divinity students in systematic theology and apologetics (1957–1986). His lectures and pastoral insights influenced a whole generation of preachers. He constructed the course of theological education in the Free Presbyterian Church which continues to serve as the basis for teaching students today. He was also a leader within the spiritual courts of the Church in a time of great theological and social change. He steadfastly opposed the lowering of biblical standards of morality. He wrote and preached against assaults on the Bible from academic theologians and evangelical leaders. He was resolute in his defence of the Lord's Day and called for a consistent witness to it in the face of widespread compromise. He was a faithful Protestant and resisted the advance of Romanism in Scotland and the United Kingdom. He made intelligent and insightful comments on the world of politics, economics, national and international affairs as well as on evangelicalism and movements within the Church of his day. Most of all however, he is remembered as a faithful preacher of the unsearchable riches of Christ to sinners.

An appreciation of his preaching

I wish to close this short biographical study with some reflections on Mr MacLean's preaching. Three features of his preaching seem to call for particular comment: authority, orthodoxy, and compassion.

Firstly there was the unmistakable authority with which he spoke. This was a scriptural authority and arose from a sense of the greatness of his responsibility as a preacher. Mr MacLean stated that there is a fear in entering the pulpit which ministers should never lose—the fear suitable to a man speaking in the name of God. In the vestry prior to preaching, he once commented that the most solemn moment of every service of divine worship for him was when he stood up and announced, 'Let us begin the public worship of God.'

Each part of the service was conducted under this sense of being in the presence of God. No one could avoid noticing the solemnity of the worship and the authority of God in the message. Even unbelievers in his audience would admit that there was no dubiety as to the force of the message given. One can still picture the powerful preaching of the gospel of Christ as the preacher with a raised arm cut the air in condemnation of sin and with outstretched arms pleaded with sinners to come to Christ. He had a powerful and melodious voice, even well into his later years, as he declared the truth of God to a silent and reverent congregation. His gestures were not contrived but followed from the weight and solemnity of the preacher's office and his message moving him to fervency and earnestness, as one standing between sinners and eternity. The recovery of that sincerity and earnestness is a sore need of the contemporary pulpit in Scotland and beyond.

Secondly, Mr MacLean's preaching was both Trinitarian and Covenantal in theology. By this I do not mean that he simply unfolded the doctrines of the Trinity and the Covenant as propositions taught in systematic theology. Rather we mean that no sermon failed to represent and unfold something of the being and the nature of the Triune God and of his works towards mankind in redemption. On one occasion after an action sermon I recall his simple reminder to me as a divinity student, 'Preaching the gospel is all about the Trinity.' Similarly he made clear the distinction between the covenant of works entered into with Adam as the head of the human race and the covenant of grace with Christ the Mediator of the elect. This distinction was often the foundation on which a sermon rested. To Mr MacLean, preaching the gospel was a declaration of the glorious work of the Covenant God.

Mr MacLean's preaching was God-centred and thoroughly Calvinistic. He never blurred fundamental distinctions in the plan of salvation, nor did he create false distinctions between the objects of divine love and the recipients of divine grace—a feature which sadly characterises much preaching today. He always traced salvation to the sovereign grace of God choosing a number that no man can number of the lost race of Adam. That lost race was described in its total depravity and ruin and its inheritance of eternal wrath. The wondrous love of God in sending his beloved Son into this fallen world as the surety of the elect, to redeem them and bring many sons to glory, was always his theme. The great work of redemption, which was wrought out by Christ at Calvary when he laid down his life for his sheep, was pressed upon his hearers as an efficacious and definite saving work, applied by the Holy Spirit in sovereign grace. One hearer in Glasgow in the 1970s recalls joyfully discovering that the weekly diet of preaching could be best summarised as a distillation of John Owen's classic work, *The Glory of Christ*, which this hearer was reading at the time.

The everlasting covenant of grace was therefore very prominent in Mr MacLean's preaching and the federal theology (which was more fully recovered in Scotland at the Reformation than anywhere else) was the only system through which he proclaimed the gospel. Most emphatic of all was his unfolding of the work of the Holy Spirit in the salvation of the sinner according to the terms of the covenant of grace. Again, this preaching is sorely lacking in the contemporary pulpit and federal theology itself is rejected by many evangelicals. Few recognise the evangelistic force of covenant theology. A decline in the orthodoxy of Reformed Churches and the lack of real spiritual power issuing in the conversion of sinners can be traced directly to the failure to preach the doctrines of grace in the context of the Covenants.

Thirdly, Mr MacLean's preaching was conspicuous for the compassionate directness with which he pressed on sinners the free invitations of Christ in the gospel. To him, preaching the free offer of Christ was not a mere theological proposition to be explained and defended. It was the essence of preaching Christ. The free offer was at the heart of his preaching the gospel—just as it is at the heart of the Westminster Shorter Catechism's statement on effectual calling, which he so often quoted. It is 'as he is freely offered in the gospel' that the Holy Spirit persuades and enables a sinner to embrace Jesus Christ. It is not so much the preacher as Christ himself *through* the preacher who offers salvation in all its glory and preciousness to sinners in the gospel. Mr MacLean's emphasis was reminiscent of such earlier divines as Thomas Boston, the Erskines, and John Colquhoun of Leith, who collectively represent the high-water mark of Scottish gospel preaching. This fundamental place given to the free offer of the gospel characterised Free Presbyterian preaching of the past and Mr MacLean was anxious for it to be preserved. He was hurt by preaching that failed in this regard and particularly so when there was to him no hint of compassion in the preacher. I recall him saying in his old age that he felt preaching was cold when sinners were addressed about a lost eternity without compassion. The kindly care he had for young people was always evident and to the end of his life he retained a burden for the rising generation to come under the power of the truth. Of equal concern to him, as it is to every faithful minister, was that the young should be kept from the floods of false teaching that had all but destroyed the gospel witness in Scotland.

Conclusion

In his old age Mr MacLean mentioned several times that he had wished to write books on theological subjects. His abilities would certainly have fitted him for that work. However this was not possible, owing to the very heavy workload given to him in all areas of the Free Presbyterian Church's witness from early in his ministry. While we may now regret the loss, we still have the privilege of access to audio recordings of hundreds of his sermons. This publication is a small sample of his sermons in written form, which will go some way to acquainting a wider audience with his preaching.

His passing on 13th August 2010 was mourned by many. Mr MacLean was the most prominent minister of his generation in his own Church and was recognised far and wide outside it as an able and powerful preacher. Those who follow him in the ordained ministry are called to labour and to be faithful to the same Master in preaching the same unsearchable riches of Christ. His death is also a solemn reminder to all who heard his preaching that they must yet give an account for the use they made of 'the preaching of the cross' by this faithful ambassador of Christ, who did not shun to declare the whole counsel of God. His preaching will always be treasured by the people of God. While he rests from his labours his memory is blessed and his works follow him.

REV DAVID CAMPBELL
Free Presbyterian Manse
North Tolsta

1 Unsearchable Riches

EPHESIANS 3:8

*Unto me, who am less than the least of all saints,
is this grace given, that I should preach among the
Gentiles the unsearchable riches of Christ.*

Lord's Day Morning, 22nd December 1996

We see that the Apostle Paul is taking a very low place among the people of God. The expression he uses is not only that he is the *least* of all saints, but that he is *less than the least* of all saints. Now he was taking that low place even though he was an apostle of the Lamb, and had a particular authority in the Church of God on account of his apostolic office. Yet through the grace of humility, this is the view he has of himself. This grace is in the souls of all the people of God. They are called 'the meek and lowly' (Psalm 25:9). Although Paul had been exalted to the third heaven, and had seen and heard things that he could not speak of to others, yet by the grace of God in exercise in his soul, this was the view he had of himself.

Now the apostles were ministers of the everlasting gospel—ambassadors for Christ—and they had a particular function in the Church of God. This function came to an end when the last apostle died. The last apostle to die was John, after he was sent to the Isle of Patmos, and when he died, the office of apostle came to an end. Of course the Church of God itself will be continued as long as time lasts—the Church of God is to last to the end of the world, until Christ will come 'the second time without sin unto salvation' (Hebrews 9:28). The office which now continues is the ministry of the everlasting gospel, which has been instituted in the church for the period from the death of the last of the apostles to the end of the church at the end of time.

This is a ministry, you see, that does not depend on the rather absurd notion that exists in the Roman Church and the Episcopal Church, that the apostolic succession is due to a succession of bishops in the Church, each one handing on the succession to the other. That is a mere figment of the imagination. Not only so, but the kind of bishops that are supposed to be in apostolic succession give no sign whatsoever that they are even among the people of God at all, or that they were ever called to be ministers of the everlasting gospel. We see here that the apostle held his office as all true ministers of the gospel do, 'according to the gift of the grace of God given to me by the effectual working of his power' (verse 7).

Now although Paul considered himself to be 'less than the least' of the people of God—and properly, as we believe all true ministers of the gospel consider themselves so—yet the fact of the matter is that he did belong to the people of God. All who are called to the ministry of the gospel are called from among the saints. Paul gives a definition of these saints in this epistle, when he addresses the epistle 'to the saints which are at Ephesus' and then describes them as 'the faithful in Christ Jesus' (Ephesians 1:1). It is those who have faith in Christ, who are united to Christ by faith, who are the saints. And here we may just remark in passing that the canonising of saints by the Roman Church is a figment of the imagination, a worthless notion. The saints to whom Paul was referring are the people of God, those who have faith in Christ—those who are united to Christ by faith, those who are coming up through the wilderness of time leaning upon their beloved, on their way to the heavenly Jerusalem.

At the present time we shall consider:
1. Paul the saint. Although he considered himself to be less than the least of them, nevertheless he was among them, and one of them. As he says

in another place, 'by the grace of God I am what I am' (1 Corinthians 15:10)—that is, I am among the people of God, I am born again, I am united to Christ by faith. As he said elsewhere, 'the life which I now live in the flesh I live by the faith of the Son of God, who loved me, and gave himself for me' (Galatians 2:20).

2. Paul the preacher: 'that I should preach'. That was his great work, to preach.

3. The content of Paul's preaching: 'the unsearchable riches of Christ'.

4. The result of Paul's preaching: 'that the Gentiles should be fellow heirs, and of the same body, and partakers of his promise in Christ by the gospel' (Ephesians 3:6).

1. Paul the saint

In the epistle to the Galatians, Paul says that God who had separated him from his mother's womb had revealed his Son in him, that he should preach Christ unto the Gentiles (Galatians 1:15,16). This is the key to the whole matter. The Christ whom Paul preached—the Christ whose unsearchable riches Paul preached to the Gentiles—was a Christ whom Paul had come to know, through God revealing that person to him.

More particularly, Paul says that God had 'separated me from my mother's womb, and called me by his grace'. Here we see the way in which Christ was revealed to Paul—he was *called* by the grace of God, or in other words he was called effectually by the grace of the third person of the Godhead, God the Holy Ghost.

Now in that call Paul had two experiences of a different nature. Both were spiritual experiences, because they came from the grace of the Holy Spirit (and there is nothing spiritual but that of which the Spirit of God is the author). The first experience Paul begins to describe when he says (Romans 7) that there was a time in his life when he was 'alive', but 'without the law' of God. At that time he paid very little attention to the claims of God's law—he was living as though the law of God did not exist. At that time he was of course dead in trespasses and in sins. And that is how sinners in this world live—without the law, and with no sense of the claims of the law upon themselves. Indeed Paul, being a Pharisee of the Pharisees, thought concerning the law that he was blameless. That showed of course his gross ignorance of the law of God. He was a rabbi, and in fact he had sat at the feet of Gamaliel, one of the great rabbis of the Jewish church. There he had heard about the traditions of the fathers—there he had learned to read the commentaries of other rabbis on the Old Testament—but in the midst of all that, he was completely ignorant of the law. He was 'without the law'.

But, he says, then 'the commandment came' and 'sin revived, and I died'. That is to say, he was arrested by the claims of the law of God. He came to see and to understand that the law was holy and spiritual and just and good—but that he was carnal, sold under sin. He was a slave to sin, and under the sentence of eternal death. The commandment came, and sin revived—sins that he had lost sight of, sins that he did not think of—they all now revived in his conscience. And what happened? He died! He found himself under the sentence of death against these sins, and he died to all hope of delivering himself from the sins to which he was a slave.

Now, conviction of sin does not unite souls to Christ. But in Paul's experience, he tells us God revealed his Son in him (Galatians 1:16). As he describes it in 2 Corinthians 4:6, 'God, who commanded the light to shine out of darkness, hath shined in our hearts to give the light of the knowledge of the glory of God in the face of Jesus Christ.' The Son of God was revealed to him in the gospel, in the light of the Word of God. This is of course how the Holy Spirit works—he opens the Word of God to the soul, so that in the light of God's Word they discern a glory in the person and in the work of Jesus Christ. As we have often remarked, and it is worth remarking again, there is a connection between these words from 2 Corinthians 4 and what we are told by the prophet Isaiah (who is sometimes called the evangelical prophet). In the 52nd chapter of his wonderful prophecy, Isaiah tells us that the face of Jesus Christ was more marred than that of any man. And then when the Holy Spirit came to work in Paul's soul, he showed him the glory of God in the face of Jesus Christ. When he took of the things of Christ to reveal them to the soul of Saul of Tarsus, he took this portion of the testimony of Jesus among others—for the spirit of prophecy is the testimony of Jesus (Revelation 19:10)—and showed to Saul of Tarsus, the chief of sinners, the glory of God in the face of Jesus Christ and him crucified—in the face that was more marred than that of any man. Paul saw that glory then and he came to know it, and he came to know the salvation that was in Jesus Christ and him crucified, and he began to discover in his own spiritual experience the unsearchable riches of Christ.

In this way Paul, like all of God's people, was brought to peace with God through the Lord Jesus Christ. Now he was among the people of God—among 'the faithful in Christ Jesus' (Ephesians 1:1), those who were united to Christ by faith which was of the operation of God. He was born again, he was a child of God, he was an heir of God, he was a joint-heir with Christ, he was saved in the Lord with an everlasting salvation. And as he tells us in Galatians, the life which he now lived, he lived by faith of the Son of God, 'who loved me, and gave himself for me' (Galatians 2:20).

But Paul also tells us of another experience. You see, all the people of God have spiritual experiences—every one of them, although some may have more than others. At any rate they all have this spiritual experience I've just mentioned—the experience of being united to Christ by faith. However, Paul had another experience which not all the Lord's people have: God who separated him from his mother's womb and called him by his grace, also revealed his Son in him for this purpose: '*that I might preach him*'. So let us now consider Paul the preacher.

2. Paul the preacher

God had a particular purpose for Paul. Paul had had other ideas. He was going to be a great rabbi, a principal rabbi. He had sat at the feet of Gamaliel— Gamaliel was his great hero, and he was going to be like him. That's what he thought when he was in darkness, when he was graceless, when he was Godless, when he was Christless. But now that he had been brought out of darkness into God's marvellous light, God made known a particular purpose for him. The God who had separated him from his mother's womb, who had brought him into this world, and who had called him by his grace, also revealed his Son in that effectual call, and with the purpose, *that I might preach him among the Gentiles.*

To preach Christ among the Gentiles—that was the purpose of God for this man. He had had his own ideas, and the same is true of all ministers of the gospel. God brought them into the world—they did not know that they were going to be ministers of the gospel—they were sinners like the rest of mankind, spiritually dead, and then they were brought through the new birth, through effectual calling, to know the Saviour. They had their own ideas of what they were to do in the world, but it was God's secret purpose with regard to them that they would be called to preach. God had this purpose for them all along—when he brought them into the world, when they were baptised as infants in the church, when they grew up. All along, God had a purpose to reveal Christ to them spiritually, and then to call them to preach.

Paul says in verse 7 that he was *made* a minister. 'The gospel whereof I was made a minister.' How? How was I made a minister? Because somebody told me that, well, it would be nice for you to be a minister, and then some other ministers made a minister of him? You remember what was said about John Kennedy, that eminent man, the minister of God of Redcastle. When he was being licensed in the presbytery of Lochcarron, there were other young men being licensed at the same time. Lachlan Mackenzie, who was another eminent servant of Christ, and who was himself on the presbytery, said, '*We* made ministers of the others, but *the Lord* made a minister of John Kennedy.' And John Kennedy's subsequent ministry proved that.

With Paul, and with every true minister of the gospel, they are made ministers 'according to the gift of the grace of God given unto me by the effectual working of his power' (Ephesians 3:7). As surely as he was effectually called by God, so he was called to the ministry of the gospel by God. These were both the work of God. As Paul said, 'unto me is this grace given'. Not just saving grace. He got saving grace in union to Christ, but now he's speaking about ministerial grace, given to him in the call to the ministry, 'by the effectual working of his power'.

Now notice the words, 'the effectual working of his power'. The call to the ministry is an effectual working of the power of the Holy Ghost. Just as surely as the call to Christ is made effectual by the Holy Spirit, so the call to the ministry is made effectual by the Holy Spirit. Now why do I emphasise this? Well, when the Saviour said, 'Pray ye the Lord of the harvest, that he will send forth labourers into his harvest' (Matthew 9:38), the words 'send forth' mean 'thrust forth'. The ministers of the everlasting gospel are thrust forth—whether Paul, John Kennedy of Redcastle, Dr Kennedy his son, or any other minister. It's not something they take upon themselves, but they are 'thrust out'. They feel an insufficiency, faced with the prospect of being called to the ministry. They are unwilling to take it on in their own strength—they would never dream of doing so. They must wait upon the Lord, that he would show them the way that he would have them go, and they are called, or sent out, to this work of the ministry of the gospel.

That being so, all their other plans come to an end. Whatever they were doing before their call to the ministry (and they may have been very pleased and content in their lawful occupation, as some of us were), once this call came, that door was closed. They were called away from that work altogether, to devote themselves entirely and fully to the work of preaching the everlasting gospel. Therefore they turned their back on their worldly prospects, and all that the world had to offer them with regard to worldly employment came to an end. It came to a complete end, because now they are to devote themselves wholly to the work of preaching the everlasting gospel. That's why ministers of the gospel do not have a secular employment. There were indeed occasions when Paul did take up secular employment—he was a tentmaker—there were occasions when the church was in such a condition that he had to engage in such work in those circumstances. But in the ordinary course of events and in the ordinary circumstances of the church, the church is called upon to supply the necessary livelihood for a preacher of the gospel. Preachers should be content with that, for they have given up the world. Moses refused to be called the son of Pharaoh's daughter, and chose to suffer affliction with the people of God rather than to enjoy the pleasures of sin which are but for a season (Hebrews 11:24,25). So it is, of course, with all the people of God—they choose to be among the people of God, and to go with them on their way to Zion—but in a particular way the preachers of the gospel also turn their backs on the world and the things which pertain to it, and devote themselves fully to the preaching of what Paul describes here as the unsearchable riches of Christ.

Now, they are given grace for this work. 'Unto me is this grace given.' They are given grace, for example, to rightly divide the Word of truth. They do not need to depend on any natural gifts they may have. It is true that the Holy Spirit sanctifies whatever natural gifts they have, to make them useful in the vineyard. But for their work they are dependent upon this grace which Paul says 'is given'. Preaching is a grace, and consequently it is the fruit of the operation of the Spirit of God. A preacher of the gospel is entirely dependent upon the grace of the Holy Spirit to lead him and guide him into the truth— to lead and guide him to those parts of the Word of God which the Holy Spirit intends to bless to souls.

The preacher is therefore dependent too on having communion and fellowship with Christ, through the grace of prayer and through the grace of meditation. Luther, that eminent preacher of the gospel, said that there were three things that made a minister. One was supplication, the second was meditation, and the third was temptation. (He's a poor minister that doesn't know much about temptation, and he won't be able to deal with the cases of the people of God in his congregation if he doesn't know about temptation himself.) But this is all bound up with the grace of the Holy Spirit which is given to preach the unsearchable riches of Christ.

If a preacher is dependent entirely on grace for the purpose of preaching, he is also entirely dependent on it for the results of preaching. Paul may plant and Apollos may water, and both may well do so by the grace of the Holy Ghost, but it is God that gives the increase—the sovereign God, the God who commanded the light to shine out of darkness. It is absolutely impossible for a minister of the gospel to give light to any of his hearers apart from God commanding that light to shine in their understanding. It's the duty of a minister of the gospel to open up the Word of God as clearly as he can, and if he does not carry out this duty he might as well stay at home and have nothing whatever to do with the gospel. The minister's duty is to open up the Word of God, by exposition of divine truth to his people, seeking indeed that they would be enlightened. But the actual enlightenment of the soul is entirely the work of the Holy Ghost, through the Word of God, and through the ministry of the gospel.

The last point I will refer to in connection with this grace is the preacher's dependence on the Holy Spirit for pointing out the sphere of his preaching. Paul was to preach among the Gentiles, and all God's ministers have their own sphere of preaching which God has chosen for them. I am rather interested in the attempts that are made by some people to make out that a man may be a preacher of the gospel, but without preaching it at all—he just writes sermons. That seems to me very strange, because Paul doesn't speak about writing sermons. He wrote the epistles, of course, by the inspiration of the Holy Spirit, but when it comes to preaching, he says that God gave him a door of utterance (Colossians 4:3). Preachers need to utter their sermons to their congregations. However, the main point is that they are appointed to some door of utterance, some particular sphere where they engage in their ministry.

Now on one hand, that sphere applies to a particular branch of the Christian church. Ministers are called to the ministry of Christ, but they exercise their ministry within a particular branch of the Christian church in the world. For example I exercise my ministry within the branch of the church called the Free Presbyterian Church of Scotland. That was appointed to me as surely as the call to be a minister was appointed to me.

On the other hand, ministers are appointed to particular congregations within that branch of the church. In this they are entirely dependent on being led and guided by the Spirit of God. If you take my own case which you all know about, I was first of all a minister in Portree for eleven and a half years, and now I'm a minister here in Glasgow, where I've been for the past thirty-six and a half years. A man needs to be convinced both of his call to the ministry and that he is in the proper place for exercising his ministry. Otherwise he'll have no comfort—he'll have no peace, and no spiritual enjoyment in preaching the everlasting gospel. These things are of great importance, and we shouldn't lose sight of them. Paul travelled around, and didn't have a congregation of his own, but this was because he was an apostle, and this was a feature of the work of the apostle which was specific to this office. Even so, the apostles had their spheres allotted to them—as Peter was the apostle to the circumcision, Paul was the apostle to the Gentiles, and so he went around preaching to the Gentiles in Ephesus, Galatia, Rome, and so on.

3. The content of Paul's preaching

Now this brings me to the content of Paul's preaching, and that is described by himself as the unsearchable, unfathomable riches of Christ.

The content of his preaching was not any notions that came into his own head, or notions that he had gathered from a university department of sociology to which he gave a Christian kind of turn (as some of the pseudo-preachers of the present day seem to do). The apostle Paul was preaching the unsearchable riches of Christ.

If we think of these riches being in a field, then it is a field without boundary, riches that can never be exhausted by searching. Or if we think of an ocean, then it is an ocean without shore, without bottom, unfathomable. Opened up to us here is a presentation of the vastness of the gospel, of the glory of the blessed God—so that Paul, however long he would be a preacher, would never reach an end of preaching the unsearchable riches of Christ. There will be no end to that. Paul's ministry came to an end, as he said himself, 'the time of my departure is at hand' (2 Timothy 4:6), and an end had come to the ministry which he had received from the Lord Jesus Christ. But there was no end to the unsearchable riches of Christ.

All these riches were hidden in the field of the scriptures of the Old and New Testaments, from Genesis to Revelation. That's where this ocean fullness was revealed and made known. Therefore, when Paul preached, he preached from the Word of God, which liveth and abideth forever. If a man has any doubts whatsoever about the inspiration and the infallibility and the inerrancy of the Word of God, he shouldn't so much as think of ascending a pulpit. He has neither part nor lot with the work of preaching, because he cannot preach the unsearchable riches of Christ without being convinced in his own soul of the infallibility, the inerrancy, and the inspiration of the Word of God.

Now the apostle has told us that when Christ was revealed to him he saw the glory of God *in the face of Jesus Christ*. The expression means the person and work of Christ. And it is there we must begin—on the fringe of the unsearchable riches of Christ. We embrace first of all his person, the person of the Son of God, the one who was rich. He was rich beyond our understanding, rich beyond compare, possessing in his divine person the fullness of the divine nature—infinite, eternal, and unchangeable, in his being, wisdom, power, holiness, justice, goodness, and truth. All the attributes of the Godhead, everything which pertains to the divine nature, were all in the person of the Son. He was the image of the Father's person, the outshining of the glory of God. So there are infinite riches there, riches of understanding, riches of glory in the person of Christ as the Son of the Father in truth and love.

Then we are told in the Word of God another part of the unsearchable riches of Christ. This person, who is the Son of God, was appointed by the everlasting Father to be the mediator between God and man, in a covenant ordered in all things and sure. Not only is he the Son of God, but he is *the Son of God who became the Son of man*. The divine nature and the human nature are united together in the one person of the Son of God—not intermixed—distinct—but united together. The human nature is still the human nature, the divine nature is still the divine nature, but they are united together in the person of the Mediator. Here are unsearchable riches in the person of the Son of God—unsearchable riches in the humanity of the divine Redeemer. For it was sinless—holy, harmless, and undefiled. It was a humanity united to his divine person and a humanity through which the glory of God was manifested in this world—and through which the glory of God is to be manifested throughout the endless ages of eternity, for the glorified Saviour is the Lamb in the midst of the throne. A view of the unsearchable riches of this glory was given on the Mount of Transfiguration, when the glory of the divine person of the Saviour shone through his holy humanity. John says, 'We beheld his glory, the glory as of the only begotten of the Father, full of grace and truth' (John 1:14). Unsearchable grace, unsearchable truth, unsearchable glory shining through the humanity of Jesus Christ. That's just setting before us part of the unsearchable riches of Christ.

But then his mediatorial office has unsearchable riches with respect to the functions of that office. Now you all know yourselves that the functions of that office are the functions of Prophet, Priest and King. The last two Sabbath days we have been dealing with the apostleship (or the prophetic office) and the priesthood of Christ. These are unsearchable.

There are unsearchable riches in the apostleship of Christ, for he has the words of eternal life. What riches are in the words of eternal life! And when he speaks these words it is by the grace of the Holy Spirit which was poured into his mouth. This is what made him beautiful in the eyes of David—'Thou fairer art than sons of men: / into thy lips is store / of grace infused' (Psalm 45:2). The grace of the Holy Ghost was poured into his lips so that he would speak the words of eternal life, and so that his people would be able to say, 'His mouth is most sweet: yea, he is altogether lovely. This is my beloved, and this is my friend, O daughters of Jerusalem' (Song 5:16). What immeasurable riches are in the Word of Christ! What immeasurable riches in the apostleship of Christ!

What immeasurable riches there are in the priesthood of Christ! Well, how can we measure them? Can we measure it in this way, by using the words which refer to the richness, the unsearchable richness, of the merit of the blood of Christ?—the blood of the divine High Priest was shed for the remission of the sins of many (Matthew 26:28). Now, here are the unsearchable riches of the blood of Christ, that the blood of Jesus Christ, God's Son, cleanseth from all sin (1 John 1:7). There are unsearchable depths in the merit of the blood of Christ, unsearchable riches in the merit of the blood of Christ. When David said, 'Yea, wash thou me,' looking to the riches of the blood of Christ, he says, 'and then I shall / be whiter than the snow' (Psalm 51:7).

And what immeasurable riches are in the intercession of Christ! The Father has given him whatever his heart desired (Psalm 21:2). There must be immeasurable riches in an intercession which contains everything that will ensure that all those who come unto the Father by him will be saved to the very uttermost. To the very uttermost! Unsearchable riches! To the very uttermost!

What unsearchable riches are in Christ as the King, as King over Zion, God's holy hill! Oh yes, this generation may despise him, but the hour is on the wing when they'll want the mountains of Scotland to fall upon them, to hide them from the wrath of the Lamb. Christ is a glorious King. His crown is a crown of glory—the Father set it on his head, a crown of purest gold. Men gave him a crown of thorns, but the Father set on the head of his glorified King a crown of purest gold. This King possesses unsearchable riches, and he possesses them for the sake and for the good of his kingdom— for the sake and for the good of those within his kingdom. The kingdom of God consists not in meat and drink, but righteousness and peace and joy in the Holy Ghost.

Now we come to this, there are unsearchable riches in the love of Christ. And that is what Paul speaks of in this chapter. Listen to his words when he prays that the people of God would be rooted and grounded in love. As Christ dwells in the heart by faith, they would be rooted and grounded in love, and being rooted and grounded in the love of Christ they might be able to comprehend, or take a view of this ocean. This unsearchable ocean of the riches of the love of Christ. And how does he measure it? He measures its length and breadth and depth and height. 'That ye may be able to comprehend with all saints'—yes, with *all* saints, including the least of them.

1. The *breadth* of the love of Christ—embracing what breadth! It'll be seen at the end of time, when they're gathered at God's right hand—they'll be from every nation, from every kingdom, from every land, from every clime,

because of the breadth of the love of Christ, embracing all the nations and those out of all nations. Princes shall come out of Egypt, Ethiopia shall stretch forth her hands to God, and all nations will be gathered around the throne, because of the breadth of the love of Christ.

2. The unsearchable riches in its *length*. Who can measure it? Who can measure the riches of its length? I have loved thee with an everlasting love. It is from everlasting to everlasting. Love that knew no beginning, love that will know no end.

3. And the *depth* of it! The depth of this love. How shall we explain the richness of the depths of this love? Well, let the Holy Spirit explain it to you. 'You know, brethren, the grace'—and the love—'of our Lord Jesus Christ, that, though he was rich, yet for your sakes he became poor, that ye through his poverty might be rich' (2 Corinthians 8:9). Here are the depths—how rich he was, and how poor he became, so that those who were poor might become rich. See, that's the wonder of it—that's part of the depths of it—the depths to which he came, the depths of the man of sorrows, the depths of the death he died on the cross of Calvary, the depths to which he sank when he drank the cup of death, until he cried, 'It is finished.'

4. And the *height*! The height to which he went himself when he rose from the dead by the power of an endless life and ascended up on high. And the heights of where he is now, at God's right hand in his glorified humanity, at the right hand of the everlasting Father, drinking in from the rivers of pleasure that are at God's right hand for evermore. Part of the rivers of his pleasure are in these words, 'He shall see of the travail of his soul, and shall be satisfied' (Isaiah 53:11). Through the preaching of the everlasting gospel, he will see those whom he loved with an everlasting love, those for whom he died—he will see them being brought out of darkness into God's marvellous light—touching the hem of his garment, and receiving the life that shall never end.

And the height also is the height to which they are to come. And that brings me just to the last point, where I must conclude: the height of his love is to take them (through the preaching of the gospel) from the dunghill and put them among the princes of his people.

4. The result of Paul's preaching

Those who were exceeding poor, he raises up in his love to be heirs of God and joint-heirs with Christ. They say themselves, 'He thought on us in our low estate, for mercy hath he ever.' This then is the result of the preaching of the gospel, brought before us here in a brief compass—'that the Gentiles should be fellow-heirs and of the same body, and partakers of his promise in Christ by the gospel.' They are heirs of these riches, and they will be searching them out in time and throughout the endless ages of eternity. How greatly blessed the people are, who know the joyful sound of the everlasting gospel preached by Paul, and preached by all the servants of God according to the grace of God given to them! In other words, those to whom Paul was sent to preach, the Gentiles, would come to be fellow-heirs with all the people of God, and joint-heirs with the Saviour. Heirs of God and joint-heirs with the one of whom we read here that his riches are unsearchable. They would be brought into the whole family of God, and made heirs of God and joint-heirs with Christ. What riches! And all through the riches of his grace, all through the riches of that salvation of which his glory is declared to be very great, the unsearchable riches of Christ.

People who are saying, 'I'm poor and needy'—they are made partakers of these riches. 'I'm poor and needy—yet of me the Lord a care doth take.' In being united to Christ by faith they are made partakers of these riches—of being saved in the Lord with an everlasting salvation. They are made heirs of God and joint-heirs with Christ, heirs of the everlasting love of the everlasting Father. That's what the Saviour prays for them: 'that the love wherewith thou hast loved me may be in them, and I in them' (John 17:26). They are heirs of that love—that is their inheritance. 'God is of mine inheritance / and cup the portion,' and therefore, 'Unto me happily the lines / in pleasant places fell; / yea, the inheritance I got / in beauty doth excel' (Psalm 16:5,6). This is the inheritance of an heir of God. They are joint-heirs with Christ of his riches, the unsearchable riches of Christ. They will be searching out these riches in time and throughout the endless ages of eternity.

How greatly blessed Paul was! How greatly blessed the people of God are! And what a blessed gospel it is to preach! How worthy it is to be preached, and how worthy it is to live for, and (as many of the people of God in Scotland believed and proved in the past) it is even worthy to die for. The unsearchable riches of Christ!

May he bless his Word. Let us call upon his name.

2 Ye must be born again

JOHN 3:7
Marvel not that I say unto thee, Ye must be born again.

<small>UNDATED, PROBABLY 1960S</small>

We have an account given here of the visit of Nicodemus to the Lord and Saviour Jesus Christ. Nicodemus was a Pharisee and a ruler among the Jews. As we see from the account given here, he came by night, no doubt so that his fellow Pharisees and rulers could not observe the fact that he was consulting Jesus of Nazareth. But the darkness of the night in which he came was not to be compared to the darkness of the heart of Nicodemus himself. Yet this is the very time when he professed to have light to teach others, as the Saviour himself pointed out to him. 'Art thou a Master of Israel, and knowest not these things?' Here was one who professed to possess the light that came from heaven in order that he might spread it abroad to others—one who read to them the Word of God in the synagogue, delivered an exhortation, and led the worship of God—yet his heart was darker than the night in which he came to Jesus.

However, we see that he did have some measure of light, in that he had to acknowledge (as his conscience made him acknowledge) that Jesus was one who gave every sign of being a prophet who had come from God. His miracles testified to that fact. We are to remember, contrary to the notions that are spread abroad by some, that during the 400 years from the prophecy of Malachi down to the appearance of John the Baptist, the Spirit of prophecy had been taken away from the Jewish church and that the power of performing miracles likewise had largely disappeared. We are told by some that in those days everybody believed in miracles, and therefore Jesus of Nazareth was able to deceive them in a way that cannot be explained. That idea of course shows great ignorance, and the fact that it is shown in those who profess to teach others to discuss the miracles as an evidence of Christianity only shows how dark the minds of some can be. The fact is that there were no miracles, or at least very few miracles, during the time between the end of the Malachi's prophecy and the appearance of John the Baptist in the wilderness of Judea. That was why John's appearance caused such a tremendous upheaval and also why the miracles of Jesus, even in the darkened heart of Nicodemus, composed an evidence that he could not resist, that Jesus was one who came from God.

We have to remember that these miracles recorded in the Scriptures give every evidence that they are true—from many positions and many points of view. There was plenty opportunity for his contemporaries to deny these miracles, but they did not. Furthermore, the miracles which the Saviour performed were intended to confirm his doctrines: if his doctrine is true, then these miracles are true. You cannot believe that Jesus of Nazareth has power to forgive sin if you do not believe in the miracles performed by the Saviour, because that was the very reason he gave for performing them, namely, 'that they might know that the Son of man hath power on earth to forgive sins'. The miracle and the doctrine are therefore bound together. What kind of thinking is behind the attitude that people take up if they are going to believe that Christ is able to forgive sin but that he is not able to perform these miracles? In fact it was far easier for the omnipotent Saviour to perform the miracle than it was for him to forgive sin, because in order to forgive sin he had to die the death on Calvary's tree, which required more than omnipotence. If people expect to have their sins forgiven and to be in heaven with Christ at the end of life's journey, while at the same time they deny the miracles—well, what the Saviour said to others could apply to them too, 'If the light that is in you is darkness, how great is that darkness!'

1. We can consider in the first place that these are the words of the Wisdom of God. It is the language of him who has the tongue of the learned, the one who came in God's great name to save. This is his declaration, 'Ye must be born again.' It should be sufficient for every one of us to believe it that he should say so and testify this to be the case.

2. Then in the second place we shall notice that this was not a marvel. Nicodemus thought it was. 'How can a man enter into his mother's womb and be born a second time?' It was a marvel to the mind of Nicodemus—it could not penetrate his mind, he could not understand it, but the Saviour said, 'Marvel not'.

3. In the last place we shall notice what he says, 'Ye must be born again.' This is a necessity, in the absence of which there is no salvation. This is a 'must' coming from the mouth of the Wisdom of God, and it must be fulfilled if we are to enter the kingdom of God, and if we are to escape the wrath and curse of God due to us on account of our sin. 'Marvel not that I said unto thee, Ye must be born again.'

1. The declaration of the Wisdom of God

These are the words of the I AM THAT I AM, Jehovah the Son of God. The miracles which he performed showed that he was a teacher come from God, in an outstanding sense of the term. This work belonged to him. John points out in this gospel that this name was given to him, not only that he is the Son of God, but that he is the Word of God—the Word that was with God, the Word that was God. This person, the Son of God, has this name—the Word of God: a name that belongs to him in a peculiar way, and a name that, belonging to him, fits him to be a teacher come from God in an outstanding sense of the term.

Now, I have often pointed out (and I point out these things again and again, because we should be seeking grace gradually to grasp them more and more)—that the Saviour is the Word of God because through him the glory of the Godhead is revealed and made known outside the Godhead. There is no knowledge of God, there is no knowledge of the mind of God, of the counsel of God, of the love of God, outside the Word of God—outside the second person of the Trinity. The Saviour said, 'No man hath seen God at any time; the only begotten Son, which is in the bosom of the Father, he hath declared him.' This is part of the glory which belongs to the person of the Son of God—that he is the one who reveals and makes known the Father in so far as that glory is made known. He is called the teacher come from God because he is the one who reveals and makes known God's glory. He makes known that glory in such a way that none can discern it apart from knowing the Son. 'He that hath seen me hath seen the Father.' This person is not a mere man, and it is not that he has grown into his knowledge of the Father, but he is one whose knowledge of the Father is the knowledge of one eternal person about another eternal person. He knows the fullness of his Father's heart, he knows the fullness of his Father's counsel, he knows the fullness of all that belongs to the Father. Therefore, he is the Word of God and he is the one who alone is able to reveal him as the teacher that comes from God.

Now, his coming from God is brought before us in a certain way. John in this gospel explains that 'the Word was made flesh, and dwelt among us.' The Word was made flesh—the second person of the Godhead, as the teacher come from God—this Word, the Son of God, was made flesh. He came from the Father in this remarkable way.

Now, it is true of course, if we look back to Moses and the prophets of the Old Testament, that Jesus by his Spirit instructed them, and by his Spirit made God known to them as the God of their salvation. Therefore in that sense of the term he came by his Spirit. I don't want to linger too long on this point, but we read that the Spirit of Christ who was in them declared the revelation that was given to them. It was declared through the Son of God, the Head of the Church of God, by his Spirit instructing them, inspiring them, to give the knowledge of God in their day and generation and to record it for us in the books of the Old Testament.

Here, Nicodemus is not confronted with Moses nor with Elias, but with one who says, 'I say unto thee'. He is the teacher come from God, the Word made flesh. He dwelt among us, or tabernacled among us. This was the tabernacle in which the Son of God was now dwelling. In former days, he had dwelt in the tabernacle in the wilderness, dwelling between the cherubim in the shekinah glory. He had dwelt in the pillar of cloud by day and the pillar of fire by night. Now he was in this tabernacle of his holy humanity, from which he will not now depart, world without end. He is the teacher come from God, the Son of God, the Word of God, dwelling in a holy humanity and speaking the thoughts of God in the words of man.

You see how near he came to this man Nicodemus. He knew the blackness, the darkness, the ignorance, the vileness of this man's heart. These things were true of Nicodemus' heart even though he thought he was going to be in heaven with Abraham, Isaac and Jacob. If he had not met the Saviour on this occasion, he would be in hell with the devil and his angels. Jesus came near and spoke to Nicodemus face to face. God had already spoken to Moses face to face, and that expression means, of course, with a greater nearness than other prophets had enjoyed. But here it is a truth, a reality. Here is the Word made flesh, near to this man, speaking to this man, saying to this man, 'I say unto thee'.

Then, this person is the Wisdom of God. No problem is too great for the New Testament Solomon. The Queen of Sheba brought her hard questions to Solomon because he was the wisest man the world had ever known. Here is one who is the Wisdom of God as surely as he is the Word of God. As the Wisdom of God, when he speaks, he speaks from infinite knowledge. And when he speaks from the knowledge of infinite wisdom, he speaks from the knowledge of that wisdom being applied in the most glorious way. Men may possess knowledge and not be very wise about using it. Scientists possess a great deal of knowledge and they are going to blow people to pieces [with nuclear weapons]. They have done that already and they are threatening to do it again. One of the great failures of the scientific world is that their knowledge is very often channelled into evil purposes and for evil ends.

But here is the wisdom of God, and all the knowledge that he possesses is channelled into this—the glory of God (and consequently for the ultimate glory of those to whom he says, 'I say unto thee').

Now, you might be ready to say, 'Well, if I had been in the world when Jesus of Nazareth was there; if I had stood by the grave when Lazarus was raised from the dead—if I had been at the wedding at Cana of Galilee when the water was changed into wine—if I had been there when the leper was cleansed—if I had been there when the miracles that Nicodemus refers to were performed—if I had been there when the man in whom the legion of devils was sitting clothed and in his right mind at the feet of Jesus—then, I would have been ready to listen.' Would you? Multitudes have not. These very miracles, and especially the miracle of raising Lazarus from the dead, occurred at the very time when people like Caiaphas were consulting to put Jesus to death. That was the effect that the miracles had on the Pharisees and the rulers among the Jews. Again, you need not say, 'Well, if I had been there at the time of Jesus I would have behaved myself differently from what I am doing now,' because Christ addresses you now in the Word of God. When the Word of God is read, when the Word of God is preached according to the mind of the Spirit of God, Jesus is saying, 'I say unto thee'.

This is one of the reasons that those who are ambassadors for Christ should declare the mind of Christ, not their own notions and ideas that float about in their own brains. Christ's ambassadors should declare what they find in this Word, that is, the Word of Christ. He is their personal Word, and this is the written Word, and therefore when the Word of God is preached according to the mind of God the Holy Spirit, Jesus is saying to your soul, 'I say unto you'. The Holy Spirit applies the Word of God to their consciences and souls, when that great and precious experience spoken of here—the experience of being born again—is fulfilled in the words of the Saviour, 'the hour is coming, and now is, when the dead shall hear the voice of the Son of God: and they that hear shall live.'

'Verily, I say unto *thee*.' This he says to Nicodemus as though there wasn't another sinner on this side of death and the great white throne. That is how

Christ speaks from his Word, and in connection with the mind of his Spirit as revealed in his Word: he is addressing *you* to whom the Word of God has come, as though there wasn't another sinner on this side of death and eternity but yourself and yourself alone. 'Verily I say unto thee.'

Now, of course, we all understand that this is a great subject and we can only touch briefly on the fringe of it, the subject of this teacher come from God. Oh, what an inestimable, what a glorious privilege to have this Master, to be a disciple of this Master, whose mouth is most sweet, who has the tongue of the learned! What a glorious privilege! to be a disciple of this Master, who is mighty before God and all the people to open the understanding, to open the Scriptures, to give us to grow in grace and in the knowledge of the Lord and Saviour Jesus Christ, who is clothed with the Holy Spirit to carry out this great work!

2. What the Saviour said was not a marvel

He said, 'Marvel not that I say unto thee, Ye must be born again.' Here was this man Nicodemus, this teacher in Israel, this man who was highly thought of, ruling over others, preaching the Word of God to others—here he was, and he did not know what it meant to be born again. That was the darkness, that was the ignorance, that was the blindness of this man. We may be ready to say that this was a marvel. Is it?

The Saviour said, 'Art thou a master of Israel, and knowest not these things? If I have told you earthly things, and ye believe not, how shall ye believe, if I tell you of heavenly things?' And this, mark you, is speaking of the new birth: an earthly thing, in this sense of the term, that it must take place on this earth, in this world. We shall never be in heaven and we shall never see the glories of heaven, unless we are born again on this side of death and the great white throne. The Saviour says to us, 'Marvel not'. We have no reason to marvel. The new birth goes clean contrary to human nature, it goes clean contrary to all that human nature thinks of, and it goes clean contrary to all the opinions and ideas that exist among men, both in the religious world and outside.

Now, the main reason that the Saviour gives here for the fact that we must be born again is, as he says in this verse beside it, 'That which is born of the flesh is flesh.' We must be born again—but here is a law operating in the souls of men which cannot be gainsaid, and which cannot be changed apart from divine power, that 'that which is born of the flesh is flesh.' By the word 'flesh' here, we are to understand human nature in its godless state. We are to understand it in Paul's terms when he says that 'in me (that is, in my flesh) dwelleth no good thing'. It refers to that human nature which you and I were born into the world with, the nature which lies at the back of the faculties of our souls, that human nature which is flesh, that human nature which is without the image of God, without the knowledge of God, without holiness, without spiritual light—human nature dead in trespasses and in sin. That's what is meant by the 'flesh', and in that flesh there dwells no good thing.

Therefore, this is the conclusion brought before us by the Wisdom of God (and would God give us grace to understand, to lay hold on it): 'that which is born of the flesh is flesh'. It is of the same nature as the nature from whence it comes. It can never be anything different. The flesh can never change in any real sense of the term, because that which is of the flesh is flesh: that which comes from the corrupt heart is corrupt, that which comes from the evil heart is evil, that which comes from the unbelieving heart is unbelieving. It cannot be anything else. It is impossible by a fixed law, due to the corruption of sin: 'that which is born of the flesh is flesh'.

This then is what explains the fact that with every breath we draw, we are sinning against God—that in everything we do, we are sinning against God. When we engage in the public worship of God with a godless heart, with an unbelieving heart, with the flesh and flesh alone, then our worship is of the flesh. This is the condition that the Saviour refers to here, in which Nicodemus was, in which you and I are, in which all the children of men are by nature. It is impossible for us to do anything else: that which is born of the flesh is flesh—it is not spiritual, it is not pleasing to God, it is not something that will make us acceptable in the sight of God. We may think, 'Well, we are not as bad as others outwardly'—and indeed we may not be. Of course, those who are bad outwardly, if they continue in sin, shall be 'beaten with many stripes' (Luke 12:47). To continue in a course of outward sin and to say, 'Well, I cannot do anything else,' as though you were not responsible for it—this idea that you just carry on in sin—is completely wrong. We must remember that sin must be accounted for, and sin is to be punished by the wrath of God, although not everybody will have the same load of the wrath of God. The fact remains that our works, though they might appear good to us, and though they may appear good to others, remain the works of the flesh. 'That which is born of the flesh is flesh,' and it can never be anything else.

Now, you see, we may say, 'Well, that applies to those who are guilty of adultery, heresy, envyings, and so on'—all the works of the flesh mentioned by Paul in his epistle to the Galatians. But you see, my dear friend, Nicodemus was a religious man—a very religious man—a very strict religious man, like Saul of Tarsus. Like the other Jews he was ready to say, 'We have Abraham for our father.' He was ready to say, 'We have the Bible. We have the temple in Jerusalem. We have the priesthood according to the house of Aaron. We have the synagogues where the Bible is read, where exhortations are delivered, where prayer is made and praise is offered to God, and indeed I stand there as a ruler of the synagogue.' But the Saviour says to him, 'That which is born of the flesh is flesh. It is of no avail in the sight of God. It is of no avail to bring you into the kingdom of God.' Similarly, he rejoiced in the sacraments. He would have been circumcised the eighth day, the same as Paul—that was one of the things that Paul as a Pharisee rejoiced in, that he was circumcised the eighth day, that he was of the tribe of Benjamin. We do not know what tribe Nicodemus belonged to, but certainly he belonged to one of the tribes of Israel and he would have thought highly of that—'a Pharisee of the Pharisees', one who was engaged in serving the God of their fathers. As he was here, Nicodemus with all his heart had the full expectation that when time should be no longer, he would sit down with Abraham, Isaac and Jacob in the kingdom of heaven above.

But the Saviour says to him, 'That which is born of the flesh is flesh.' All of that arises from the old nature—the old nature dressed up in religion, the old nature dressed up as a Jew, the old nature dressed up as a teacher, the old nature dressed up as a Pharisee. That which is born of the flesh is flesh, and does not ascend any higher, however great the zeal may be. Look at the zeal of Saul of Tarsus, going round throwing the people of God in prison. His zeal was outstanding in the kingdom in which he was—which he thought was the kingdom of God—but it was all of the flesh.

You see, this is one of the grave dangers in which people stand. They lose sight of what the Saviour says here, 'Marvel not that I say unto thee, ye must be born again'—and so they go about dressing up the old man, making the old man a religious man and exercising carnal zeal and carnal religion under the cloak of the hope of going to heaven. But the Saviour said, 'That which is born of the flesh is flesh.' He can never rise above his old nature, he can never be pleasing to God, and he cannot bring his soul into the kingdom of God.

3. The necessity of the new birth

Therefore, you see the need of the new birth. 'That which is born of the flesh is flesh, *and that which is born of the Spirit is spirit.*' Something spiritual must be brought into the soul—a new nature must be brought into the soul. There must be a change of nature in the experience of the sinner, so that he has what is spiritual in his heart and mind—so that he has 'the spiritual mind which is life and peace'—so that he is born of the Spirit of God, and is living, not dead. The reason why the Saviour said, 'Marvel not that I say unto thee, ye must be born again,' is because of the absolute necessity of this change of nature. Unless a man is born again, he cannot see the kingdom of God. It cannot be done. It is absolutely impossible.

That means too, that unless a man is born again, he cannot see the King of the kingdom. We were speaking this morning on the words, 'Thine eyes shall see the King in his beauty.' Now, you cannot see Christ in his beauty unless you are born again. The reason for that is that there is no such thing as faith in the flesh. The flesh can never bring forth faith. You see, one of the great objections that I have to modern evangelism is that it encourages a most dangerous form of religion, one which comes from the flesh. For Billy Graham to say to some poor creature who does not know his right hand from

YE MUST BE BORN AGAIN

his left in connection with the things of the Spirit of God, 'Now you say this prayer after me,' and he gives them some prayer to say, and then he says to them, 'You are born again'—what kind of religion is that? And then these people take up a Christian profession, and especially the young people: they take up a Christian profession, then they begin to go to the crusades, then they join the choirs. They have the kind of religion which is purely of the flesh—that is not the new birth. But the new birth is absolutely essential. You see this is the very reverse of what Billy Graham believes. He says, you believe in Christ and then you are born again, but the Saviour says, 'Except a man be born again, he cannot see the kingdom of God.' He cannot see the King of the kingdom, and he cannot have faith, until he is born again. Faith is the first exercise of the living soul, the soul that is born again: a living soul exercises living faith in a living Saviour. But what does modern evangelism teach us? That a dead soul exercises faith in a living Saviour and then it becomes alive. That is a delusion. What the Saviour says here is, 'Marvel not that I said unto thee, Ye must be born again,' because if we are not born again, we cannot see the kingdom of God, and we cannot see the King of the kingdom.

Now, as you remember, the Saviour says, 'Every one which seeth the Son, and believeth on him, may have everlasting life' (John 6:40). He says the same thing in his intercessory prayer to the Father, 'This is life eternal, that they might know thee, the only true God, and Jesus Christ, whom thou hast sent' (John 17:3)—the Greek word there means, 'this is eternal life, *in order that* they may know thee, the only true God.' You cannot know Christ unless you are a living soul, and that is just what he is saying here. You cannot know the Father in Christ and you cannot come into possession of eternal salvation unless you are born again.

Unless we are united to Christ by faith, our relationship to God is one of condemnation—our relationship to God is that we are the children of wrath—our relationship to God is that we are under the sentence of death. That's what the Saviour says here. Mark his words well: 'He that believeth on the Son hath everlasting life: and he that believeth not the Son shall not see life; but the wrath of God abideth on him' (John 3:36).

49

Surely that is clear enough. Could words be clearer than that? Unless we come to see Christ and believe on him and see him with the eye of faith and see with the eye of our understanding and trust him with all our hearts, we cannot be saved. We cannot come out from condemnation. We cannot have our sins (which are many) pardoned. These blessings are only for those who are in Christ—for *them* there is no condemnation. We must be born of water and of the Spirit if we are to be united to Christ by faith, and if we are to be inside that kingdom which hath no end at all.

Now, what does it mean for a sinner to be born again? to pass from death to life? Well, the Saviour says here, 'The wind bloweth where it listeth, and thou hearest the sound thereof, but canst not tell whence it cometh, and whither it goeth: so is everyone that is born of the Spirit.' Now sometimes when references are made to this verse, the application is made that there may be strong gales in the experience of the soul and in other cases they may be brought into the kingdom more smoothly. Now, that does not apply to this verse at all. What this verse is referring to is the breath, just a slight, gentle breeze, which cannot be predicted. People can tell when there is going to be gales. If you ask the fishermen out in the North Sea or in the Faroes what they are doing at certain periods of the day, they will tell you that they are listening to the weather forecast, to see if any gales are forecast—because gales *can* be forecast. But what is referred to here is the breath of wind that is so gentle that when it goes through a tree you only know it's there because the leaves begin to shiver in the breeze. *That* is what the Saviour is referring to here.

What's brought before us here is the sovereignty of God the Holy Spirit. He is sovereign in his work, and he is sovereign with regard to those who are born again by his divine and gracious power. You find that again and again. Take the instance, 'I will be as the dew unto Israel' (Hosea 14:5). Who can control the dew? Who can cause the dew to fall? No one! That is the work of God the Creator. And so with regard to God the Holy Spirit—his coming, his going, his workings—his work is altogether sovereign. Yet his work is also bound up with the means of grace in this world, and one of the great doctrines for which we stand as a church, along with other evangelical churches worthy of the name, is that no one can be born again without the Word of God. We are not speaking of infants who die in infancy, nor those who are without their reason, but we are speaking in the general case of those who are in possession of their reason. It is absolutely fundamental that they are 'born again, not of corruptible seed, but of incorruptible, by the Word of God, which liveth and abideth for ever'.

At one time, about ten years ago, when I was going to Rhodesia, there was a missionary on the boat. He was very indignant with me because I did not go to hear a woman from the Salvation Army who was preaching, and who he thought was a very good preacher. He came to remonstrate with me because I did not go to hear her. Of course I told him that I would not go to hear her for the simple reason that the Lord never asked her to open her mouth. The Lord never spoke through her because he never gave her authority to preach. This made him more indignant, and he went on to say that he believed that Christ could reveal himself to anybody anywhere, without the Word of God at all. So I asked him then, what was he doing, as a missionary, carrying the Word of God to Natal? You see, if it is the case that people can be converted apart from the Word of God, apart from the gospel of the grace of God, then why preach it? No, people cannot be converted apart from the Word of God. 'Faith cometh by hearing, and hearing by the Word of God' (Romans 10:17).

The movement of the Spirit of God is described here in these highly significant words, 'The wind bloweth where it listeth, but thou canst not tell whence it cometh, and whither it goeth.' However, you can tell that it has been there by the effect that it has—when you saw the leaves begin to shiver in the trees, you knew that this gentle breeze was passing through. So it is with regard to the Holy Spirit. He comes and he goes. He comes according to the sovereign pleasure of God. He comes in virtue of the blood of Christ that was shed for the remission of the sins of many. And when he comes and breathes on the Word of God, it has an effect in the soul of a sinner. I am sure that some of you here know exactly what this means. There are times when the Word of God has an effect and times when the same words have no effect. Why? Because the wind bloweth where it listeth. There was a godly man from Ness in Lewis, Malcolm Macleod. On more than one occasion he told of the time he was in Dingwall at a communion and he went out to pray, he enjoyed a great deal of the presence of the Lord. So he made up his mind he would come back the next year to the same place, but when he went, he found it empty. Why? Because the wind bloweth where it listeth, and thou canst not tell whence it cometh and whither it goeth.

It is bound up with the new nature being imparted to the soul of a sinner that the Word of God is made effectual in convincing the soul of sin and misery. And the Word of God is also made effectual in presenting Christ to the soul as the Saviour who is able to save to the uttermost. This gentle breath is seen in the soul of the sinner. It is seen especially in the will of the sinner— making the sinner willing to receive Christ, and to rest upon him alone for salvation as he is set forth in the glorious gospel of the blessed God.

Therefore, the soul that comes to embrace Christ by faith does so in virtue of the new birth. It does so because a new nature, a new principle, has been imparted to that soul. That which is spiritual now comes to have a place in that soul (and the Holy Spirit is the author of all that is spiritual). You see how Paul says the same thing when he is speaking about the new creation, 'If any man be in Christ, he is a new creation: old things are passed away; behold, all things are become new.' And what else? 'All things are of God' (2 Corinthians 5:17,18).

The Holy Spirit is the author of all that is spiritual. The third person of the Godhead, in the name of Christ, is the author of all that is spiritual—of all spiritual prayers, of all spiritual meditations, of all spiritual preaching and all spiritual hearing. The Holy Spirit is the author of all of this. In the light of this, the Saviour says, 'Marvel not that I say unto thee, Ye must be born again.' What a tremendous change is effected by the personal presence and power of the third person of the Godhead!

You see, that is, of course, one of the great things with regard to the preaching of the gospel. It's not, my dear friend, by might, nor by power. It's not by the power of men, nor by the eloquence of men, nor by the earnestness and zeal of men, that sinners are born again. 'Not by might, nor by power, but by my spirit, saith the Lord of hosts' (Zechariah 4:6). If you are born again by the Spirit of God, then you come to see and to value Christ—Christ is made precious to you, and you come to find in him pardon for sin, and peace with God, and the hope of everlasting life, and the hope of being with Christ at the end of life's journey.

That is a hope worth having, and it is a hope which the born again sinner does have—however often it may be tried, however difficult it may be on many occasions for him or for her to think that they are going to be with Christ, when they still find within them so much of what is born of the flesh, even though they have crucified the flesh with its affections and lusts. In the day when they were made willing by Christ's power, they took the hammer and the nails and they nailed their flesh to the cross. They thought, perhaps, that it would never rise again, but crucifixion is a slow death, and the flesh will be there with them until they are made perfect in holiness—until they go to be with Christ, which is far better. There they will know and there they will understand, in a way that they never understood in this world, what the Saviour said to Nicodemus, 'Marvel not that I say unto thee, Ye must be born again.'

George Whitefield, the evangelist, as he went around from place to place, often preached on the same texts, and this was one of them, 'Marvel not that I say unto thee, Ye must be born again.' Once, somebody asked him, 'Why do you preach so often on that text?' and his answer was, 'Because ye must be born again—that is the reason.' And if that new birth does not take place, whatever else we possess or think we have, 'that which is of the flesh is flesh'.

May he bless his Word. Let us call upon his name

3 The wise and foolish virgins

MATTHEW 25:1-13
Then shall the kingdom of heaven be likened
unto ten virgins, which took their lamps, and
went forth to meet the bridegroom.

LORD'S DAY EVENING, 2ND JULY 1978

Towards the close of this chapter, the Saviour is discoursing about the day of judgment. It is a fact of divine revelation that there will be a day of judgment. And our conscience also gives witness that there must be a day of judgment. By the conscience we mean the ability to pass judgment upon our acts and our thoughts, as well as upon the acts and thoughts of others. The very fact that we possess consciences makes it plain that the God of eternity is also one who can judge, and who is a judge. And the Scriptures reveal to us that the day of judgment which shall come at the end of the world will have as its judge God in the person of the Son in our nature. In other words, the judge of the world is the one appointed by God and he is the Lord and the Saviour Jesus Christ. Therefore the scripture says that we must all appear before the judgment seat of Christ.

When the Saviour speaks here of that day, that momentous day, that day of indescribable solemnity, that day of the most solemn and dreadful issues, we ought to hear what he has to say. He is the one who is going to judge, he is the one who will appear, no longer in a state of humiliation, but in the glory of his Father and with the holy angels. He is the one who will separate the sheep from the goats, and he is the one whose voice will be heard saying on the one hand, 'Come, ye blessed of my Father' (verse 34), and on the other, 'Depart from me, ye cursed' (verse 41).

Now, the Saviour, prior to speaking of the day of judgment, enforces on his hearers the great necessity of personal piety. He enforces on his hearers—and on us to whom the Word of God has come—the absolute necessity that we should have what will stand at the day of judgment, and the absolute necessity that it should be personal. We should understand that as we die and go into eternity alone, so the issues of death and judgment are concerned with each one of us separately and alone. The piety that we possess must be of this nature, that it will be personal, that it will be real, that it will stand when the Bridegroom comes. Whether we take that to be the day of death (as we do on this occasion), or whether we take it (as we might) to be the day of judgment, the fact remains that the whole weight of the parable of the ten virgins and the parable of the talents is to impress upon us not only the solemnity of judgment, but also the absolute indispensable necessity that we should have true piety—that we should have saving grace—that we should not fail of the grace of God—that we should not be left to be like the five foolish virgins here, who came near to the kingdom of God, but discovered too late that the door was shut.

Now of course there are many issues raised by this parable and it is not my intention at the present moment to deal with them all, but rather to deal with those that will be in accordance with what I've been endeavouring to say, the absolute indispensable need of personal piety. You see, there is no question of us borrowing piety from others. That was part of the folly of the foolish virgins, that they wanted to borrow oil from the wise. They said to the wise virgins, 'Give us of your oil; for our lamps are gone out,' or as the Greek word means, our lamps are going out. But the wise virgins had none to spare. On the day of judgment, or even at the day of death, no one will have anything to spare. There will be no piety loaned from the father to the son—there will be no piety passed on from the mother to the daughter. Each one must possess it for himself and for herself, and it must be real.

With regard to the marriage that is brought before us here, there is some discussion among interpreters as to the actual incident, and some difference of opinion arises from the various views taken of the Jewish marriage.

1. The expectation of the virgins

We take the view that the particular part of the marriage which is being referred to in this parable is the journey of the bridegroom with his bride to the bridal home. These virgins were waiting for that bridal procession— they were waiting for the bridegroom to come, and waiting to hear the voice of the bridegroom as he conducted his bride on her way to the bridal home. They were waiting to join that procession, and waiting to go in with them. The bride is not mentioned here, however. That is because sinners are represented by the virgins. That is a common device in these parables, and also in Psalm 45, where the one described as the Bride, or the Church, is spoken of as the virgins—describing the whole by referring to the individuals. That is what we are stressing here—the individual necessity for individual personal piety.

2. The folly and wisdom of the virgins

Some five of them had these expectations fulfilled and five of them did not. So in the second place we shall notice the wisdom of the wise and the folly of the foolish. In my judgment the actual numbers themselves do not mean a great deal, except that they stress the fact that those who started off together, as they were all virgins together, and all together had their measure of oil, were separated in the end. The five of them who were wise had ensured that their piety was personal. They had ensured that they had something that could not be taken from them, and something that would give them light to enter in to the bridal home, and to be with Christ and his people (which is far better), whereas the foolish did not possess that.

3. The outcome

Then in the third place we shall notice what happened. The Saviour says, when the bridegroom came and the wise had entered in, then the door was shut. So the Saviour says, 'Watch therefore, for ye know neither the day nor the hour wherein the Son of man cometh' (verse 13). There is this great and indispensable necessity of having this personal, genuine piety that will take us in before the door is shut. If we have this kind of piety, it will mean that instead of a shut door there will be an abundant entrance into the kingdom of heaven. At a time in our congregation when the Bridegroom has come to us as a congregation and has removed one—one whom we believe was one of the wise virgins—how tremendously necessary it is for us to learn from this the absolute—the indispensable—necessity of personal piety of a real nature.

1. The expectation of the virgins

Now the first view brought before us is of the bridegroom on his journey, taking his bride to the marriage home, while these virgins were waiting to join the marriage procession.

This brings before us that eternity will reveal what are the real issues in what is happening in this world. Not the meeting of the United Nations, not the meeting of this politician and the other politician, not the industrial disputes, not the economic circumstances, not what the papers are full of. Rather, as day follows day, and month follows month, and year follows year, and generation follows generation, Christ is taking his Bride to the marriage home. Christ is taking his Bride to his Father's house. As he said, 'In my Father's house are many mansions: if it were not so, I would have told you. I go to prepare a place for you. And if I go and prepare a place for you, I will come again, and receive you unto myself; that where I am, there ye may be also' (John 14:2, 3).

And although the world doesn't know it, and although the newspaper world and the world of radio and television don't know it, this is taking place. The world loves their own, and they take notice of the deaths of those who are popular in the world, but they don't take any notice of the people of God when they go to heaven. But in time, day after day, generation after generation, this is taking place, that Christ is gathering his people and conducting his Bride on her way to the Father's house.

That brings me to notice now, in connection with this divine Bridegroom, that he was going to the Father's house. It was said of this Bridegroom that, having loved his own who were in the world, he loved them unto the end. He knew that he came from God and that he was going to God, and we must always remember that both his coming from God and his going to God were bound up with the love that he had to his Bride. He came from God and he went to God out of the love that he had to the children of men, a number that no man can number. He came from God—he was God the Son—and he came from God in this sense of the term, that he came to be in the world, to serve for them and to win them for himself. You remember that remarkable occasion when he washed his disciples' feet. He laid aside his garments and put on a linen cloth and began to wash the disciples' feet, taking the place of a servant in order to do this duty for them, and saying to them, 'Except I wash you, you have no part with me.' This was symbolising and setting forth that he was and is the eternal Son of God, that he became man, and that he became man out of love to sinners of mankind.

And as God-man he went to God. Having loved his own which were in the world, he loved them even to the end. He came from God and he went to God, and he went to God as the God-man. He went to the Father's house as the God-man, and his journey was a journey through Gethsemane and Calvary, a journey through the grave's devouring mouth. In this journey he accomplished the redemption of his people, and it was all done out of love to them. 'He that hath the bride', says John the Baptist, 'is the bridegroom' (John 3:29). He had the Bride in his heart of everlasting love and he purchased his Bride with his life, with his own precious blood.

What he is doing in this world now, as the pleasure of the Lord prospers in his hand (Isaiah 53:10), is to gather in his Bride. The nations are but the small dust of the balance in the presence of God (Isaiah 40:15), and as they wonder about their ideas, as they exchange their notions, as they advance the vanities of their own minds, this work is going on: Christ is gathering in his Bride, and he is conducting her, one soul after another, to the Father's house. One by one, they are being washed in his precious blood, regenerated by divine grace, and at death being made perfect in holiness, to go in to the Father's house, 'that where I am, there ye may be also' (John 14:3).

Now, you see, the view brought before us here is that these virgins were waiting for the bridegroom. Jesus of Nazareth was to pass by, as the divine Bridegroom of the church, gathering his people down through the ages of time. And here they were, these virgins, and they were waiting to join the procession, to go in to the Father's house. They were waiting to join the procession, and enter in with Christ and his people to everlasting glory. That's what they were expecting.

I mentioned this morning already that one of the distinguishing features of godly fear in the heart of any sinner in this world is love to the worship of God. In the book of Revelation we read of those who followed the Lamb whithersoever he went, and one characteristic of them was they had not defiled themselves with women, for they were virgins (Revelation 14:4). This is a pointer to the fact that they love and delight in the worship of God. In that respect they were virgins—they delighted in the purity of the worship of God, and they delighted to engage in the worship of God as pure, and in accordance with the Word of God.

And you must notice that the ten were virgins, every one of them. All ten of them delighted in the worship of God, and the purity of the worship of God. They would be grieved if they found something impure in the worship of God, or if they found something in the doctrine which was contrary to the mind of the Holy Spirit. But as well as being attached to the worship of God, it was also necessary for them to have lamps, and to have light in these lamps. This was necessary in order that they might join the procession, so that each one would have her own light to bring along on the onward march of the Church of God. They were waiting to join their lamps and their light to the procession that was going to the house of the Bridegroom. Their lamps represent their profession—they were professing to be virgins, they were professing to be waiting upon the Lord, they were professing to be attached to the Bridegroom, they were professing to be attached to the Bride—they were professing that, when their time would come, they too would as it were add the light that they possessed to the marriage procession.

2. The folly and wisdom of the virgins

That brings me to the second point, that five of the virgins were wise and five were foolish. The wisdom of the wise is described in this way, that they had oil in their lamps, and that in fact they had a sufficiency in oil in their lamps, so that when, as it happened, the call came at midnight, when it was dark, their lamps did not go out. On the other hand, while the foolish did have a certain measure of oil, their light began to go out. The measure of oil that they had was not sufficient when the midnight call came. Instead of the light shining out, when they came to trim their lamps, they had the dreadful realisation that their lamps were going out. 'Our lamps are going out!'

The Word of God in several places uses oil as a symbol for God the Holy Spirit. For example, oil was mingled with aloes, myrrh and cassia and poured on the head of Aaron (and carried the aloes, myrrh and cassia down to his garments). The oil there was a symbol of the Holy Spirit. Therefore we have brought before us here the necessity of having a work of the Holy Spirit. All these virgins were attached to the worship of God, professing an attachment both to the Bridegroom and to the Bride, and professing that their great desire was to join the bridal company and 'be brought with gladness great, / and mirth on every side, / into the palace of the King' (Psalm 45:15). But in order for that to be truly the case, they needed oil. Because they had oil, they had light in their lamps. In the case of the five wise, because of the measure of oil they had, the light that was in their lamps would never go out. But in the case of the foolish virgins, at the very time that they needed it most—at midnight, the darkest hour, when they needed this light as they never needed it before, and at the very time that the Bridegroom's voice was heard—they discovered that their light was beginning to go out.

Now this brings before us a great and most necessary truth, that we must make our calling and election sure. As the apostle says in one place (2 Corinthians 13:5), 'Examine yourselves, whether ye be in the faith.' It is a most necessary exhortation, 'to make your calling and your election sure: for if ye do these things, ye shall never fall' (2 Peter 1:10). In other words, what is stressed here is the absolute, indispensable necessity of having the saving work of the Holy Spirit, evidenced in the saving light of saving knowledge of the divine Bridegroom. That's what the wise virgins had. They had oil in a measure that ensured that they would be ready, however dark the night may be, and however sudden the call of the bridegroom might be. They had enough oil to ensure that they would be ready to join the procession, that they would be ready to go in, so that for them, the door would not be shut.

So we have this distinction made, a most important distinction, between the oil that the wise virgins had, which was the oil of the Holy Spirit in his saving operations, and the oil that the foolish virgins had, which was the oil of the Holy Spirit in his common operations. That had light as well. You see, these two things are of tremendous importance, although nowadays one of the most serious and dreadful things that's taking place is that so many people mistake the common operations of the Holy Spirit and the light that proceeds from that, and confuse it with the saving operations of the Holy Spirit and the light that proceeds from that. You can see that for yourselves if you survey today's religious scene, although I'm especially emphasising just now the necessity for us to be concerned about this for ourselves, to be really concerned about our personal, individual piety, as to whether or not we ourselves personally have been made partakers of these saving operations of the Spirit of God.

Now what does the oil of the Holy Spirit in his saving operations consist of? Well, the light of the lamps in this parable points to the saving knowledge of the Bridegroom. We must remember that Christ came into the world to save sinners. 'This is a faithful saying, and worthy of all acceptation, that Christ Jesus came into the world to save sinners,' says Paul, 'of whom I am chief' (1 Timothy 1:15). Therefore, the saving operations of the Holy Spirit, the oil of the Holy Ghost dwelling in the lamp of the soul, involve a saving knowledge of sin. We have to stress this because it is very necessary—it was never more necessary than it is in the day and generation which you and I live, where the light and flighty religion of the foolish virgins is a fashionable one, where people think they're going to heaven, and they're going to find the door shut. But the Word of God tells us that when the Spirit of truth comes, he will reprove the world of sin—he will convince the sinner of sin. He does so by shining the light of his Word into the sinner's soul and giving the sinner to see their sin. 'In that purest light of thine / we clearly light shall see' (Psalm 36:9)—and one of the things we shall clearly see is our sin—'My sin I ever see' (Psalm 51:3).

That's where personal piety begins. It's not a question of seeing the sins of others (although if you see your own sins, of course in a sense you will see the sins of others), but you see, where this holy oil is, where the saving operation of the Holy Spirit is, this is made personal—a stern, unshakable reality, that 'my sin I ever see'. I see my sin separating between me and God, separating between me and the people of God, separating between me and the Bridegroom. Sins that are innumerable, sins that cannot be numbered or counted, rise up in the spiritual experience of the soul, so that he is convinced that in him there dwelleth no good thing (Romans 7:18). He is convinced of this also, that it is impossible for him to deliver himself, impossible for him to set himself free, impossible for him to obtain the pardon of sin by any ways or means of his own. And also, he is convinced that it is impossible for him to receive this Bridegroom in the exercise of natural strength, in the exercise of natural wisdom, in the exercise of natural knowledge.

Therefore this knowledge of the Saviour is spiritual. It is knowledge of a Saviour who saves, a Saviour whose name is called Jesus, for he shall save his people from their sins (Matthew 1:21). As Christ says with regard to the Holy Spirit, 'he shall glorify me: for he shall receive of mine, and shall show it unto you' (John 16:14). In that faculty of your soul which is your understanding, the Holy Spirit reveals to you Christ as the Son of God, Christ as the God-man, Christ as the one who died for the ungodly, Christ as the one who rose again, Christ as the one who loves sinners, Christ as the one who said in the exercise of his grace that 'him that cometh to me I will in no wise cast out' (John 6:37). This is the Christ that sinners get light upon. This is the Christ that the sinner receives and embraces in the exercise of saving faith.

Where that is, it will be a characteristic of this person, that with all his spiritual exercises, or with all her spiritual exercises, they will always be concerned to know, are they saving exercises? Are they from the Spirit of God? Are they the experiences of the people of God? This is what the wise virgins did—they made sure of this, they made sure that this piety was personal. They made sure that they had Christ for themselves.

You see, whatever doubts a soul may have—and God's people may, and do at times, have doubts—yet they know (and they have no doubt whatever about this) that they must have Christ for themselves—they must receive him personally, they must have him for themselves and not for any other. They must have him for themselves, and they cannot even receive him for anyone else—they cannot receive Christ for their families, much though they would wish that their families would themselves receive Christ.

They realise—and they go on realising this more and more—that they need Christ for themselves. The nearer they come to the end of life's journey and the great white throne, the more they see the need that they should have Christ for themselves—a saving knowledge of this divine and glorious Redeemer. That saving knowledge is spiritual, and it is living. As the Word of God declares, 'Then shall we know, if we follow on to know the Lord: his going forth is prepared as the morning' (Hosea 6:3)—which is to say, that this is a growing knowledge. They desire to grow in grace and in the knowledge of the Lord and Saviour Jesus Christ. They are concerned to have this oil, this light, so that if the call came at midnight and they went to join the marriage procession, then they would have this light—light to see the Bridegroom, light with which they could see the procession of the Bridegroom and the Bride and those who are with them, going into the Father's house. That is what the people of God will have at death. 'The Lord's my light and saving health, / who shall make me dismayed?' (Psalm 27:1). In the valley of the shadow of death this light will not fail them. Even in the valley of the shadow of death they can say, 'Thou art with me; thy rod and thy staff they comfort me' (Psalm 23:4). This is what lightens the valley of the shadow of death— the knowledge that they have of Christ. The Christ who they will meet on the other side of death is the Christ who loved them and whom they knew in this world. 'They that know thy name, in thee / their confidence will place: / for thou hast not forsaken them / that truly seek thy face' (Psalm 9:10).

The foolish virgins had light too, but it was not light that sprang from the saving operations of the Holy Spirit. Instead it was from the common operations of the Holy Spirit, the common strivings of the Holy Spirit. The great difference between the two is that the one effects a *change* of nature, the other effects a *restraint* of nature. In the sinner who has the common operations of the Holy Spirit, there's no change of nature—he's not a new creature in Christ Jesus at all. Just by the common operations of the Holy Spirit he or she may have times of being disturbed about their sins, times when they think that they have Christ, and think that they are looking to Christ and trusting in Christ. They are just like the stony ground hearers: they believed in the Saviour, they had joy in their believing, but these were just the common operations of the Holy Spirit. One of the signs of that was their superficiality. They were not concerned about examining themselves to ascertain whether they were of the faith—they were not concerned to have the Holy Spirit in his saving operations—as long as they had some religious feelings of one description or another, that was enough. Their religious feelings brought them to church and perhaps brought them to the prayer meeting, and perhaps at times they felt moved in their hearts under the preaching of the gospel—but they never truly came to know the Saviour. They never come to have saving light upon the person and work of Christ. They never come to taste of the love that had no beginning and that has no end. Yet for all that, they mingled with the virgins who were wise.

Then a trial was imposed upon them all. The bridegroom tarried. At one time they all seemed to be ready—their lamps were trimmed and their lights were burning. But the bridegroom tarried. While there was this delay, both the wise and the foolish slumbered and then they slept. What a solemn thing, my dear friend! How very solemn it is, in the day in which we live, when the steps of the Bridegroom are seen so little, when so little sign of the footsteps of our God and our King are seen in the sanctuary! What danger, what tremendous danger there is, that we should first of all slumber and then that we would sleep, wise and foolish together! That's what happened in the parable. The Bridegroom tarried—the hours began to pass—the expectations began to dim—the flesh was proving stronger than the spirit—they began to slumber and then they began to sleep.

You see, my dear friend, that this is what is happening in our day and generation. As Christ tarries, the Church ought to be responding by earnestly inquiring, 'O the hope of Israel, the Saviour thereof in time of trouble, why shouldest thou be as a stranger in the land, and as a wayfaring man that turneth aside to tarry for a night?' (Jeremiah 14:8). When the footsteps of our God and our King in the sanctuary are not seen as they were in days gone by, and although we pray for it and long for it, yet the Bridegroom tarries, let us be careful that we do not slumber—and worse, that we do not sleep. That happened to both the wise and the foolish, those who had saving grace and those who had common grace. Great sleepiness prevailed among all the virgins, all those who were waiting for the marriage procession to come, who were waiting to join it with their lamps and their lights burning, and who at one time had been waiting with great expectation. But now, you see, when the Bridegroom tarried, other things began to come in. Other things began to blunt their expectations, began to blunt their spiritual appetite and dim their spiritual light. They began to slumber first of all, and then they slept. They all did that: the wise did that, the foolish did that too.

That can happen in both cases, you see. This isn't merely something that affected the foolish virgins. The Scripture tells us that those who are under the common operations of the Spirit may endure for a time, but when persecution arises for the Word's sake, then, because they've got no depth, then of course they just collapse and their profession comes to an end (Mark 4:5, 16, 17). But here you have those who truly do have saving grace, and they are in the same danger of slumbering and sleeping. Perhaps this danger arose partly from mixing with the foolish virgins and giving them a place in the Church that they shouldn't have, but whatever was the cause of it, they all slumbered and slept.

As we have often remarked, the Lord tests the profession of every one, and very often he tests the profession of people on the very point where their profession seems strongest. Think of the case of Peter. With courage he drew the sword in the garden—he cut off the servant of the high priest's ear—he was quite prepared to fight the matter out with the enemies of Christ, and if necessary to die with him. That's what he said, although he wasn't allowed to do that. But then, you see, when he came to be tested, when he came to go into the sieve of Satan, he was tested on this very thing, on his attachment to the Saviour. It wasn't Roman soldiers that he was confronted with, or people with staves and lamps, but only a maid. When she challenged him that he was with Jesus of Nazareth, he denied that it was so, and denied the Saviour. This was the very man who shortly before had been saying that he was willing to die with him. Here he was tested on the very profession that he had made.

Now you can see the same thing with the virgins here. They're tested on the very thing that they professed. Their lamps are burning, they're waiting joyously for the bridegroom and the bride and the bridal procession going to the house of the bridegroom. They should have been the ones who were awake, they should have been looking with expectation, they should have been straining their ears and their eyes for some sign of the coming of the bridal procession. But instead of that, their eyes were closed, they slumbered, and then they slept.

3. The outcome

When the midnight call came, 'The bridegroom cometh!' then the wise virgins realised their condition. They began to trim their lamps. You see, my dear friend, saving grace will secure this. As the Saviour says to Peter, 'I have prayed for thee, that thy faith fail not' (Luke 22:32). The faith which has its origin in the anointing oil of the Holy Spirit would not fail, even though he denied his Saviour, and although he followed him afar off. This was to preserve him: the possession of saving faith and the prayer of the Saviour 'that thy faith fail not'. Here in the parable, when the midnight call comes, they are awakened—they realise that their lamps need to be trimmed, they realise that the hour is come, and the oil preserves this for them.

Of course, we must be careful here. We do not want to imply that a Christian doesn't need to be watchful. We would be the last to ever suggest such a thing, or to give the impression that this excuses any Christian for failing to be watchful. Quite the opposite! The Saviour says, 'Watch therefore.' The fact that saving grace will secure that they will never perish is not a pillow to be put under the head of a slumbering wise virgin. We are not to give any suggestion of licence for that, and may the Lord prevent us forever from putting pillows under any head of any soul on the way to eternity. Nevertheless it was the case that the wise virgins had something which the world could not give them, and something which the world could never take away. So they began to trim their lamps.

'Go ye out to meet him.' All the virgins rose and trimmed their lamps. Even the foolish recognised that they were not ready, and they recognised what was worse: that when they came to trim their lamps, to take away that which would becloud the light, instead of the light shining, they discovered, 'Our lamps are going out!' *Now* they recognise the difference between them. Before, they had perhaps despised the wise virgins. Perhaps they had thought that they had more light than they had, that they had more security than they had, that they had more assurance than the wise virgins had. But now the solemn reality was that their lamps were going out. The knowledge of the Saviour which they professed to have would not endure when the Bridegroom came and when they were called to go out to meet him. They recognised now that the wise virgins had something that they themselves did not have. Now they wanted to share it, but they were too late.

It's all very well for you just now to despise the people of God. It's all very well for you just now to say this and that and the other thing about the wise virgins who are attached to Christ and to his worship and to his cause and his people. But the hour is on the wing when you'll wish that you had what they had. When the call came, the foolish virgins would have given the world for some oil from the wise virgins. In fact they even thought that it was something that they could purchase from the wise virgins, and of course they were told, 'Go ye rather to them that sell, and buy for yourselves.' That is part of the parable. This oil cannot be bought—and at any rate they were too late to go. But in any case, the point I would like to stress just now is how they felt. They wanted to have what the others had. 'Give us of your oil,' they said. Oh! They realised now that they did not have it after all. The people of God had it—*their* lamps were not going to go out in the valley of the shadow of death—and they would like to have it too. 'Give us of your oil.'

'Not so,' the wise virgins said, 'lest there be not enough for us and you.' It cannot be done. No one can give you saving grace, my dear friend, not even when they are dying themselves. They need it all, and they need it in the article of death, they need it as they join the marriage procession to the Father's house. And that is what happened when the call came. 'The bridegroom came; and they that were ready went in with him to the marriage.' They joined the marriage procession, they went in with the procession into the house of the Bridegroom, into the Father's house. They were ready, because saving grace had secured that they were ready. The power of the Holy Ghost in his saving operations had secured this to them. This is what they had desired and this is what they prayed for on many an occasion, that they would be ready when Christ came. Ready they will be, when the time comes. That will be secured for them. They'll have the oil to die as they were given the oil to live. They'll be given the light of the knowledge in their understanding as they enter into the light of everlasting glory, and they will know the Lamb in the midst of the throne, the Lamb whom they embraced by faith, the Lamb of whom it is said, 'Unto you which believe he is precious' (1 Peter 2:7).

But you see, on the other hand, the others discovered that they did not have enough oil—they discovered that their lights were going out—and when they came, they discovered what was even worse, that the door was shut. We are told here, 'The other virgins came.' Ah, what solemn words! The foolish virgins came, and they were so foolish they did not realise the door was shut, and that it was shut now for ever and for ever. 'Lord, Lord,' they said, 'open to us.' But he answered and said, 'Verily I say unto you, I know you not.' There it is: 'I know you not.' They never came to the knowledge of him, and he never knew them. He never had fellowship and communion with them, he never loved them, he never gave himself for them. Now they have discovered it, and they discovered it when it was only too late. There was no open door now, for ever and ever.

You can see now what I said at the beginning—the absolute necessity of personal reality in religion. The kind of atmosphere of our generation is togetherness—multi-national, bulk-buying, everybody together—and it all contributes to a lack of personal responsibility, a lack of actual, personal dealing. People deal in groups, or in trades unions, but relatively speaking there is little emphasis on individual responsibility. Well, my dear friend, here it must be personal, it must be real, it must be between you and Christ. It's not between you and the minister—it doesn't matter what the minister or the elder thinks of you. It has to be between your soul and Christ, so that you will know him and that he will know you—so that you will have fellowship with him, and this light of spiritual knowledge of Christ, so that you cannot but love him and you cannot but embrace him, and so that when the midnight call comes, you will be ready and go in to the marriage.

On the other hand, there are those who just presume. On the part of the foolish virgins, this was presumptuous sin, and it is a terrible thing. Sin at all times is a terrible thing, but presumptuous sin is a more awful thing still. You are presuming upon God, presuming upon Christ. You cannot do that! And this is where this necessity comes in. Watch therefore, for in such an hour as ye think not the Son of man cometh. We should be seeking that the Lord would bless to us not only his Word, but the voices by which he is speaking to us in his providence when his people are being taken away. They are ready and they go in to the marriage, and if you and I are to follow them—if you and I are to be with them and with Christ—then we must be among the wise virgins. It will be part of our wisdom in our day and generation to take care that we do not slumber and that we do not sleep, but that we be awake and watchful, for ye know not when your Lord cometh.

May he bless his Word. Let us call upon his name.

4 Make your calling and election sure

2 PETER 1:10
Wherefore the rather, brethren, give diligence to
make your calling and election sure: for if ye do
these things, ye shall never fall.

LORD'S DAY, 19TH AUGUST 1984

In writing this epistle by the inspiration of the Holy Spirit, Peter is giving
advice to those who have obtained like precious faith with himself and
the other apostles. That is to say, they were Christians who were living a
life of faith upon the Son of God. He is pointing out to them the necessity of
continuing in that life and growing in that life.

Brought before us here is the fact that having the grace of faith (which
secured their eternal salvation) was only the beginning of the life of godliness
in this present world. Now that they had begun, they were to go on to grow
in the life of godliness, and the particular way which he mentions here is, by
giving diligence to ensure that the various other graces are added to the grace
of faith.

This is the way to an assurance of calling and of election. It is very often
a troubling matter to the people of God as to whether they have been called
and whether they are elected. The way to come to the assurance of both
calling and election is not only in possession of the grace of faith to begin

73

with, but in growing in the life of godliness—in adding these other graces to the grace of faith. They are to add virtue, knowledge, temperance, patience, godliness, brotherly kindness, and charity. This is a sure and certain way of coming to a solid and comfortable assurance with regard to election and with regard to calling.

Now, of course, assurance is something to be enjoyed by the soul. God is sure of the elect and he is sure of those who are called. There is no question on the part of God, no doubt on the part of God, as to who the elect are and who the called are. There is no way of making the matter of electing or calling surer as far as God is concerned, because he already has infinite knowledge, he already is sure with regard to both the matter of election and the matter of calling. But the assurance mentioned here is making sure *to the soul*, in the soul's spiritual experience in this life. The soul is to be given an assurance with regard to election and an assurance with regard to calling. That is confirmed by the order in which the Holy Spirit sets it down here: to give all diligence to make their calling and election sure. This comes to the believer in this order, first calling and then election. But with God the order is different: it is election first of all, followed by calling.

1. God's order of dealing with souls
2. The soul's experience
3. Giving diligence to make calling and election sure

1. God's order of dealing with souls

From the point of view of God, the order is that election comes first and calling follows. That is the order. And there is no need for God to be assured about these matters. He is perfectly assured on both, for he is the one who has made the election, and he is the one who has effected the calling.

Now the doctrine of election is one of the fundamental doctrines of God's Word. Without election there would be no salvation for any sinner. The Word of God makes it perfectly plain that all have sinned and come short of the glory of God, and also that there is no desire in the human heart (in its ruined and sinful condition) to return to God. So if there was any question of the sinner returning to God, if there was any question of the soul being saved from sin, then that must arise in the heart of God. It certainly will not arise in the sinful, dark, ignorant soul of man. Now therefore the Scriptures also make it plain that God has elected some to everlasting life. The whole mass of mankind was in a fallen condition, in a ruined condition, under the sentence of death. God out of his mere good pleasure, in the exercise of his sovereign grace and mercy, made choice of a number that no man can number of the human family, choosing them unto salvation and to everlasting life. They were chosen.

Now, the Word of God teaches us that the electing of sinners was a particular act of God the Father. They are 'elect according to the foreknowledge of God the Father' (verse 2). This exercise of love, exercised freely, in a sovereign way, not because of any necessity outside of himself, but entirely because of his own will and his own good pleasure, is brought before us in the Word of God as an exercise of love on the part of God the everlasting Father.

According to the Scriptures, those who are thus elected to everlasting life and salvation were chosen in Christ before the foundation of the world. That means that they were chosen in Christ with this in view, that Christ would work out salvation on their behalf for them. So, as we read here, this precious faith is obtained through the righteousness of God and our Saviour Jesus Christ. And in these words the salvation that Christ wrought out is described as righteousness. He is Jehovah Tsidkenu, the Lord our righteousness (Jeremiah 23:6). It was necessary for him to work out this righteousness for his people in order that they might be saved in him with an everlasting salvation and come to taste of the love of God.

Now the righteousness of Christ is a complete garment, a garment without seam. Yet, for the purposes of viewing it by faith, as it is presented in the Word of God, we often make a distinction between two parts of this one righteousness. The first part of the righteousness which Christ wrought out we call his active righteousness. That part of his righteousness has respect to the law of God, which requires of mankind that they should love the Lord their God with all their heart and life and soul, and their neighbour as themselves. This requires love rendered by way of obedience to the law. Now that is something which the people of God could not do, because they were sinners. That is something which sinners of mankind can never accomplish, no matter how hard they would strive. Even if they did strive, they could never satisfy the claims of the law of God with regard to their rendering loving obedience to that law: and there can be no salvation for any sinner unless the claims of God's law are met with regard to obedience to that law. The Lord Jesus Christ, the Son of God in our nature, came in, taking the room and place of his people: he was born of a woman, he was made under the law, in order that he might give satisfaction to the law of God by way of rendering obedience to that law.

The active obedience that Christ rendered was such an obedience that he magnified the law and he made it honourable. The law of God never got such obedience before, and will never receive such obedience again. When Adam was in a sinless state he rendered obedience to the law of God, and that was the obedience of a man, and a sinless man at that. But when Christ rendered obedience to the law of God, it was the obedience, not of a mere man, but of the God-man. All the merit and all the dignity of his divine Person and his holy humanity united to that divine Person was involved in obedience to the law of God. Therefore the obedience of Christ is sufficient for a number that no man can number of the human race, as far as satisfying the law of God with respect to obedience is concerned. By that active obedience Christ obtained life for his people. The language of the law of God is, 'the man which doeth these things shall live by them' (Romans 10:5). And therefore when Christ the Son of God obeyed the law of God in the room and place of his people, then he obtained life for them—life that shall never end. The obedience which he gave to the law of God in the room and place of his people is what we call his active obedience.

Now the second part of the obedience of Christ we call his passive obedience. By that we mean his obedience in suffering, and his being obedient unto death. Now that was necessary because the sins of those whom he came to save deserved eternal death. That death was treasured up in the cup which the Father gave him to drink. In obtaining this righteousness, on which their salvation was to be based, it was necessary for him to die the death which the law and justice of God required. And moreover that he would die it perfectly, so that that death he accomplished would be a death so perfect that when he would cry on the cross 'it is finished', there would be no more debt left with respect to the sins of his people. And therefore he abolished death—he made an end of death—the death that was due to his people, he made an end of it through dying himself. This was his passive obedience.

These two aspects of the one obedience—his passive obedience and his active obedience—satisfy all the claims of the law and justice of God. Christ's obedience did away with the death due to their sins and obtained for them the life that shall never end. Now when we view it in this way, the only thing that we've got to be careful about is to remember that during the whole time of Christ's obedience to the law he was suffering, and further, when he was dying he was active. That is to say, he was not 'passive' in the sense that is sometimes used for being *inactive*. By being passive we mean suffering, and in his sufferings he was *active* in the sense that he was actively offering himself. He was actively offering himself in love, offering himself to the claims of the law and justice of God in love to his people. So, provided that we keep this before our minds, the idea of the two aspects of Christ's obedience is a safe way of looking at the fullness of the righteousness of Christ—the salvation which Christ wrought out, whereby he obtained eternal salvation for all the elect. They were saved in him with an everlasting salvation. When he died on the cross their salvation was secured, it was sure in him with respect to all who are in the election of grace.

2. The soul's experience
So it is clear that as far as the elect are concerned, God the Father knows who they are. But the Lamb's book of life is closed to us—we cannot look into the counsels of God to discover whether or not we are elect. Nor has he

revealed in his Word who they are. That is to say, they are not revealed in person, although, as we shall come to notice, they are revealed with respect to their character. So we must come to the second part of this matter: that it is possible to be assured of salvation, and that it comes in the order of calling first, and then election.

God who elected his people, and saved them with an everlasting salvation, also calls them. They are called. Those who are in the election of grace, for whom Christ died, are in time effectually called by God the Holy Spirit. God knows who they are, and therefore when they are effectually called, the Holy Spirit is sent to them as those who are in the election of grace. But as far as we are concerned, we must come to the experience of effectual calling and then, through coming to the experience of effectual calling, we come to discover whether or not we were in the election of grace. That is the order from our side. From God's side, election goes before calling—from our side, our knowledge of calling precedes our coming to the knowledge of being among the election of grace.

Therefore when he says here, 'give diligence to make your calling and election sure,' he begins with calling because it is there that we must begin. All those who are in the election of grace, all those for whom Christ died, all those for whom Christ has prepared a righteousness, every single one of them are effectually called in this world by the Holy Spirit. And therefore Paul in writing to the Hebrews says with regard to the holy brethren that they are partakers of the heavenly calling (Hebrews 3:1). As he says here, they are partakers of the divine nature. They are partakers of the divine nature through the promises of the gospel, that is, through the heavenly calling. So the author (or agent, if you like to use the word) of this calling is the Holy Spirit, the third person of the Godhead. No less a person is required, no less power is required for a sinner to be effectually called.

And when the Holy Spirit is imparting this new nature to the soul, we are told here that 'there are given unto us exceeding great and precious promises'. This indicates the instrument whereby the Holy Spirit effectually calls sinners to Christ. The instrument is the Word of God, and in particular the gospel and its great and precious promises. Those who are effectually called have experiences with regard to the Word of God. When the Holy Spirit is effectually calling a soul through the Word of God, the soul feels an effect, and that effect is felt with regard to the Word of God. It is very important that it in effectual calling the sinner feels the effects of the Word of God. That's what he or she feels in their soul.

In effectual calling the Word of God has a particular effect upon the person. Those who are effectually called have a saving experience of both law and gospel. That was one of the great strengths of Luther—that's how he overthrew Popery, by his powerful preaching of both the law and the gospel. Both need to be preached. Now in effectual calling the effect of the preaching of the law is 'the knowledge of sin', as we are told in the Word of God (Romans 3:20). Every one of those who are effectually called have this knowledge, from God the Holy Ghost, through the Word of God—the knowledge of sin. The Saviour himself calls the work of the Holy Spirit the work of 'reproving the world of sin' (John 16:8), or giving conviction of sin. From the Word of God, the Holy Spirit gives the soul some views of God—views of God's holiness, his justice, his purity—some views of God as the God against whom the soul has sinned. You see, David must have had some knowledge of God when he said, 'Against thee, thee only, have I sinned' (Psalm 50:4). This is part of what takes place in effectual calling: the Holy Spirit imparts to the soul such a knowledge of God as brings the sinner to see that all his sins are against God—against a holy, just God, against a glorious God. The soul sees his sins in the light of who God is. In coming to this knowledge of God, they come to the knowledge of their sins—of what sin is, of the evil that is in sin, of the bitterness that is in sin. They learn that it is an evil and a bitter thing to have sinned against God. That becomes a sorrow to them, and they are brought to acknowledge to God, 'Against thee, thee only, have I sinned, / in thy sight done this ill.'

But they also feel an effect in their souls with regard to the gospel, the promises of the gospel. That is what we have here, 'whereby are given us exceeding great and precious promises, that by these we might be partakers of the divine nature'. The gospel has its place in effectual calling as well as the law. It is in the gospel, and in the promises and invitations of the gospel, that the soul comes to be called. By the knowledge of sin they feel their darkness —'He out of darkness did them bring, / and from death's shade them take' (Psalm 107:14). They feel their sin and darkness, but the call of the gospel comes in the promises and invitations of the gospel which demonstrate and make known the righteousness and the salvation that is in Christ. In the gospel they are called on to come to Christ for salvation—to come unto him that they might have rest, to come unto him that they might have peace, to come unto him that they might have pardon, to come unto him that they might be saved with an everlasting salvation. That call reaches them. It encourages them, it draws them, so that they come to Christ. As Christ himself said, 'no man can come to me, except the Father draw him' (John 6:44), and the Father draws him by the cords of the gospel through the operation of the Holy Spirit.

Now in that way the sinner comes to see who Christ is—that he is the Son of God in our nature. The sinner comes to see a little of the work that he did, a little of the salvation that he wrought out, a little of the love that he manifested in dying for sinners. By this call of the everlasting gospel, the sinner is now drawn to come to Christ. It is in connection with that call that we see 'they have obtained like precious faith' (verse 1)—the same faith as Peter had, the same faith as all the people of God have ever had. There is no faith, you see—or rather I should say, there's no such precious faith, as it is referred to here—apart from the call. Apart from effectual calling, this faith does not exist.

One of the great dangers of modern evangelicalism, and modern evangelism, is that the impression is often given that the sinner has the capacity for faith himself—all he has to do is decide for Jesus, or commit himself, or some such phrase. The distinct impression is given that this is something that he can do himself. But those who are called effectually know otherwise. It was because of the call, the call coming with divine power, that the sinner came to have some knowledge of Christ, his person, his work, his love, his grace, his willingness to receive the sinner. This is all brought before the soul of the sinner by the Holy Spirit, who, secretly working in the soul, draws the sinner and makes the sinner willing to come to Christ.

When he's willing to come to Christ, then that is faith. Faith is the soul that's laden with iniquities coming to Christ. That is what faith is. And it's precious faith. Coming to Christ—coming to Christ with nothing to pay, coming to Christ with nothing of their own, coming to Christ in the everlasting gospel, embracing Christ in the everlasting gospel—that is where this calling leads the soul. This calling brings the soul to Christ, to embrace Christ, and wherever there is a sinner who has embraced Christ, then that sinner has been born again—made a 'partaker of the divine nature' (as we read here) according to the power of God. 'According as his divine power hath given unto us all things that are pertain unto life and godliness' (2 Peter 1:3). It is by this divine power, this divine unction of the Holy Spirit, that they are brought to exercise faith in Christ—to close in with Christ in the glorious call of the everlasting gospel, freely, without money and without price, so that they become united to him and they are clothed with his righteousness. Their sins (which are many) are forgiven them, and they become heirs of God and joint-heirs with Christ.

Now, where that is there is life. The grace of faith is the first exercise of the life of godliness in the soul. There is life—that is a living soul, a soul that has life. And Peter says here to living souls, 'Give all diligence to make your calling and your election sure.' Now assurance of election embraces what we've been endeavouring to say, our knowledge of the effects of the Word of God upon us in bringing us to a saving knowledge of Christ.

3. Giving diligence to make calling and election sure
We go on now in the third place to notice that where there is life, there must be and there will be growth.

Wherever there is a root, there will be fruit. The root of the life of godliness bears the fruit of faith. Peter is going on to say here that living souls are to concern themselves with growth in grace. By being diligent in the matter of growth in grace, they will come more and more to the assurance of their calling.

Now, when he says 'Give diligence', he does not mean that we are capable of exercising this diligence ourselves. This diligence is something which he requires of them, but in exercising that diligence we are not to forget that it is God who 'worketh in you both to will and to do of his good pleasure' (Philippians 2:13). If it is his good pleasure that the believer should will and do this duty (of adding to his faith virtue and so on) to grow in grace—and that is true—this is in accordance with God's good pleasure—then he will work in us to that end. So we are to be diligent in pleading and seeking grace to grow in grace.

That includes having a view of what growth in grace means in practical terms, so that we are not just filled with abstract, befuddled notions of what grace is. Peter outlines that for us here. 'Now,' he says, 'add to your faith virtue.' Now faith, in embracing Christ, denies any merit in the works of the person exercising faith. We often say—and it is a good word—that faith is a *self-denying* grace. That is to say, it is in the nature of faith to deny self—to deny that the soul has anything good in it. It is in the nature of faith to deny that the works which the soul may perform have any virtue in them with respect to salvation. But at the same time, the fact remains that we are to add to our faith virtue. Though faith is a self-denying grace, denying all merit to any works of ours to secure salvation, at the same time we are to have virtue. Now, virtue here means moral excellence. That is to say, while the person who has faith is to be careful to deny that works are of any value with regard to their salvation, nevertheless their conduct and life in the world has to bear this stamp of virtue, this stamp of moral excellence—or if you like to use another word, holiness.

That is the meaning of 'virtue' here—moral excellence, uprightness of character, integrity of character. Integrity of character is something that they are to grow in—they are to add that to their faith. The faith by which they receive the salvation of Christ with nothing to pay is nevertheless to be added to in this respect, that there is to be in that person a moral excellence. If they are going to be partakers of the divine nature, then there is a moral excellence in God, a righteousness, a holiness. In his first creation, man had this holiness, when he was created in the image of God: the image of God consisted in knowledge—yes—and in righteousness and in true holiness. Righteousness and true holiness—that is what we mean by virtue, this moral excellence. There should be a stamp of godliness on the soul, a stamp of integrity, a stamp of God-likeness, and the living soul should be growing in this way of integrity and moral uprightness in its life and character and activities.

Then, they are to add to virtue knowledge. Knowledge flows from virtue. Virtue is moral excellence, virtue is a moral conduct that's excellent, and as Christ himself said, he that doeth these things shall know that these doctrines are from God (John 17:7-8). People may have plenty knowledge in the world and not have moral excellence at all. In fact that is one of the great problems in the world at the present time, that there is a great deal of knowledge but there is not the moral character behind that knowledge to make it useful to the human race. Knowledge of nuclear power, for example, could be very useful to the human family, but where there is not virtue behind it, all that knowledge may very well be to the ruin of the human family. For all the talent, all the brains, all the knowledge, if they lack virtue, then that knowledge will not be beneficial either to the individual or to the human family at large. But this is also eminently true in the spiritual sense: there must be moral excellence in order that there may be spiritual knowledge of God. And the more there is of this moral excellence or integrity in the soul, that is absolutely bound up with growing in the knowledge of God.

Then to knowledge they are to add temperance, that is, sobriety or self-control. That is very necessary again, in order that knowledge may be of benefit to the human race. Natural knowledge may be of benefit to the human race, but there must be sobriety with it. In the present day there is the possibility of bringing children into the world by the use of medical science, which has raised questions of ethics in medical circles, but there must be sobriety. There must be soberness of mind with regard to knowledge, because if there is not sobriety with regard to knowledge then the person is in danger of being carried away by their knowledge. So there must be this temperance, this sobriety, this restraint. And I think that that also means that the knowledge should not be merely head knowledge, but it should be spiritual knowledge. Head knowledge of religious matters is apt to carry people away, but if the knowledge is spiritual it will be humbling. Knowledge that is not spiritual 'puffeth up' (1 Corinthians 8:1), but the knowledge that is spiritual humbles.

That's one way in which knowledge is connected with temperance and sobriety. By this knowledge, I am not only referring to the knowledge of God's nature, but also knowledge of God's ways of conducting himself towards the human family—that requires sobriety. Another instance of how this restraint is needed is seen in the friends of Job. You see, they had plenty knowledge, and much of what they said was true, but they did not have this sobriety or restraint, and when they were interpreting the ways of God to Job they went astray, and they were rebuked by God for it..

Then they are to add to temperance patience. The grace of patience is needed. Now, you can see how this flows down from faith. Faith is a waiting upon the Lord, and patience is a waiting upon the Lord in a time of suffering. Through faith and patience they inherit the promises (Hebrews 6:12). It is appointed to the Lord's people in this world to have tribulations. 'In this world ye shall have tribulation,' they are told (John 16:33), and therefore it is very necessary for them to have the grace of patience. They've got to add it—it's got to be brought into exercise in their spiritual experience. So that as their knowledge grows, and sobriety bound up with it—a balanced knowledge—then this patience comes in. As they come to know the ways of God, they are patient to wait till the hand of God reveals itself, until the hand of God brings about their deliverance.

And to patience, he says, add godliness. That is God-likeness. If they are partakers of the divine nature, if they have the new creation within them, then as they grow in grace and in the knowledge of the Lord and Saviour Jesus Christ, so they grow in godliness. There are various ways in which godliness manifests itself—in love to the law, love to the gospel, love to the truth of God, love to the cause of God, love to that which is pure, that which is upright, that which is holy. That is godliness. The divine light which is hidden down in the depths of the soul springs up in this way—in a godly life and conversation. Godliness loves the law of God. As the Saviour himself said, 'If ye love me, keep my commandments' (John 14:15). The law of God is loved by God, and therefore if you have godliness, if you are a partaker of the divine nature, then you have love to the law of God. Your desire and prayer is that you would run in the way of God's commandments, through his enlarging your heart to this end.

And to godliness, add brotherly kindness. God loves his people, and where there is godliness, there will be love for the people of God. Here is a mark of this calling, that we know we have passed from death to life if we love the brethren (1 John 3:14). This is a mark of godliness, that as God loves his people, so the one in whom is the life of God manifests his spiritual life by love to the people of God. Kindness, brotherly kindness, kindness to the people of God, love to the people of God. They are to grow in that grace—it is to be cultivated—they are to pray for showers of grace in order to cultivate the grace of brotherly kindness and love to the people of God. That is part of the life of godliness in the world.

To brotherly kindness, add charity. Charity here means what we often describe as compassionate love to the world. You see, the Lord's people have spiritual love to God's people, but they also have compassionate love for the world that lies (where they were themselves) in sin, in misery, under the sentence of death. They have a compassionate love as part of the life of godliness. You see God's compassionate love, in that he causes the rain to fall and the sun to shine on the just and the unjust, and he manifests all the benefits of his providence even to those who themselves have no grace. So the godly have this charity, this compassionate love for the world that lies in sin and iniquity. Their prayer ascends to heaven that the Lord would visit them with his salvation. They have this compassionate love—love not only to the people of God, but also love to the world that is lying in the grasp of sin and under the power of Satan.

Now you see, there is a wonderful line to be traced through these graces. They begin with faith. Faith is the leader of the graces, and love brings up the rear. Love to his people and love, compassionate love, to those who are without God and without hope in the world. This wonderful line of graces should be worn by the gracious soul as a necklace. Just like pearls are strung together for people to wear around their necks, so these graces are strung together to beautify the soul. Faith is the leading grace and love brings up the rear, for faith worketh by love, and all these graces that are mentioned here—the integrity of character, the restraint, the patience, the knowledge, the brotherly love and the compassionate love—they are all shot through with the grace of faith that worketh by love. Faith is the leading grace and all these things are in the life of godliness.

Now, he goes on to say, 'if these things be in you *and abound*'. Of course these things are in them, because they're included in the life of godliness that's in them, but what Peter is saying here is not just that these things are in them, but that they *abound* in them. That's what he's talking about— giving diligence to make their calling and election sure, giving diligence to have these graces abounding in them, being active in them, growing in them. 'They make you that you shall neither be barren nor unfruitful in the knowledge of our Lord Jesus Christ' (verse 8). There it is again, you see— knowledge attained to in gracious exercises, knowledge attained to, not by reading books, but in gracious exercises of soul.

'For he that lacketh these things is blind, and cannot see afar off, and has forgotten that he was purged from his old sins' (verse 9). This refers to the kind of person who thinks, 'Well, if I've believed in Christ then I'm saved, and that's all that's to it, there's nothing more to it.' Someone like that may imagine that he was purged from his old sins, but he's mistaken. If he's not concerned to grow in grace, he hasn't got the life at all. 'Wherefore the rather, brethren,' says Peter, and that's what he comes to now, instead of thinking like this, 'give diligence to make your calling and election sure, for if ye do these things, ye shall never fall.' Here is the way to be delivered from falling. The way to have our feet delivered from falling and our eyes from tears is in the diligent cultivation of these graces in the faculties of the soul.

It is in making their calling and election sure that people come to the assurance that they have been called—as they exercise the graces of the Spirit in a gracious way, and as they grow in the knowledge of our Lord Jesus Christ. It is in making their calling and election sure that they come to the assurance that they are not of the world, but that they are among the godly, that they have a life in their souls that wasn't there before, and a life that came to them through the call of the everlasting gospel. That life is demonstrated and exercised in their spiritual experience with regard to their growing in the knowledge of the Saviour. This is how they come to an assurance of their calling, an assurance that they are called, that they have been united to Christ, that the Holy Spirit did call them effectually, did work the grace of faith in their souls.

Now, all who are called effectually and come to a measure of assurance with regard to that calling, they also have this assurance following that— assurance of election. No one is called but those who are elect. They may be called by the outward call of the Word, and many things may take place in their lives, but they are not vitally and savingly united to Christ, and so life in their souls, the life of godliness in the exercise of these graces (as we have been endeavouring faintly to explain), is not there. But where that life is, in the person who has been effectually called, then that is an assurance to them that they are in the election of grace. It's an assurance to them that Christ died for them. He died for none but the elect, and if they are effectually called, then Christ died for them. So you see this is the way to come to assurance of election. It's not by way of seeking to get special revelations from God, special signs that we are among the elect. That won't get you anywhere—it will only bring you into greater darkness. Rather it is this—to give diligence to make your calling and election sure. It is to discover whether you have been effectually called, and if you reach a measure of assurance in that, then it follows, as night follows day, that you were loved with an everlasting love and that you were chosen in Christ before the foundation of the world.

That's the way to come to it, and that's what Peter is teaching here in this chapter. The way to come to any measure of assurance of our election means coming to a measure of assurance of our calling, and if we get that, then we have a measure of assurance of our election. That's why, when the Holy Spirit is speaking to Christians of this matter here through Peter, he puts it in this order, first your calling and then your election. This is the order in which to obtain assurance: assurance of calling leads you to assurance of election. That's the proper way, and that's the only way, and that's what Peter is teaching here. An assurance of calling means our being assured in some measure that we have been called effectually, that we've come to Christ, that we've come to know what it means to exercise faith in Christ and to be seeking to grow in godliness and in the graces which we have mentioned here, and the other graces described in the Word of God.

As I said already, we must always remember in connection with seeking to grow in grace that it is God who works in you both to will and to do of his good pleasure. It is he who does this work, secretly and powerfully, by the Holy Spirit. But that does not excuse us for lack of diligence. It's just in the same way as if you take a simple thing, say like the commandment, 'Remember the Sabbath day, to keep it holy.' We're required to obey that commandment, but we need grace to do it, and we also need diligence. There's no use breaking the Sabbath day and then saying, 'Oh, I didn't get grace to do it.' That's not Christianity at all. But it means that on the Sabbath day you're seeking for grace to keep the Sabbath day holy. The same thing applies to all the requirements of God in his Word. His grace is sufficient for us, his strength is made perfect in weakness. This is the way in which we come to a solid and a comforting assurance that we were loved with an everlasting love—that we come first to an assurance of our calling and then this will follow.

May he bless his Word. Let us call upon his name.

5   Christ the Priest

EXODUS 28:2
*Thou shalt make holy garments for Aaron thy
brother for glory and for beauty.*

Lord's Day morning, 23rd December 1990

In these chapters in Exodus, along with chapters in Leviticus and Numbers,
we read of how the worship of God was set up under the Old Testament
dispensation, the covenant that God made with the nation of Israel at Mount
Sinai.

That form of worship was according to the mind of God. For God is not
to be worshipped according to the ideas that may enter the minds of men.
That is one of the great lessons that we need to understand in our generation.
Although we now live in the New Testament dispensation, we are still to
understand that God is not to be worshipped according to the ideas of men.
He has clearly indicated in the New Testament dispensation the way that he
is to be worshipped. The reason for that is that the Lord our God is holy still.

In the worship of the Old Testament tabernacle, there were three forms
of ministry. There was the ministry of the Levites, which was confined to the
court of the tabernacle. There was the ministry of the priests, from which
the Levites were excluded, which was carried on in the Holy Place. There
was also the particular ministry of the High Priest on the Day of Atonement,

which included his entering into the Most Holy Place. All this was intended to impress upon the minds of those who worshipped the God of eternity that our God is holy still, and that those who draw near to him need to realise this, and need to be in a proper frame if they are to worship him according to his mind.

But we can see how perverse our generation is, in the way that they delight in a religious observance that has no authority from the Word of God, that is, the so-called Christmas, and yet at the same time, they are engaged in fresh breaches of the Sabbath day, which does have divine authority as a day that is to be kept holy. Then again, there is a spirit of perverseness when people say that no civilised society would have capital punishment as the penal sanction for one who takes the life of his neighbour, although capital punishment has the sanction and the authority of God and the Word of God. Yet some of these very same people are quite prepared to see thousands upon thousands upon thousands of infants slain in the womb. But God is holy. He is not to be mocked. Whatsoever men sow, that shall they also reap. Therefore while a way has been opened to worship God, those who draw near to him must always remember that when they do so, they are drawing near to the holy one, the high and the lofty one, the God of infinite power, the God of inflexible justice, although also the God whose delight is in mercy.

Now the first lesson that is taught here in connection with the worship of God is that we need a priest. Of course, we don't need human priests—they are finished with. (The priesthood of the Church of Rome is a perversion of the office of the priest, as so many doctrines of the papal Church are—a perversion of Christianity.) The days of the priesthood of Aaron are over and done with for ever and ever. But Aaron was a type of the Priest who is a priest for ever, namely, the Lord and Saviour Jesus Christ, who is a Priest for ever according to the order of Melchizedek.

1. The need for a priest

We shall notice first of all the need there is for a priest in order that we may worship God in spirit and in truth. The need of a priest arises from the solemn, stern, unshakeable reality that we have sinned against God. All have sinned and come short of the glory of God. Our sins and our iniquities have separated between us and God, and that separation will be eternal unless we are delivered from our sins by Christ Jesus. When he was born into this world he was given a name, and his name was called Jesus, for he shall save his people from their sins. And when people begin to discover the awfulness of being a sinner, they will begin to understand the preciousness of Christ. But until then, they have no idea, no conception. Fanciful ideas they may have. They may write hymns. They may write poetry. They may preach so-called sermons. They may make a great noise about him at this time of year. But Christ was never precious to any soul until that soul came to know (by the inward grace and power and teaching of the Holy Spirit) that he had sinned against heaven and in God's sight. By our sin we are excluded from the worship of God. And therefore a priest is needed in order to bring sinners into the presence of God. But in order to bring sinners into the presence of God, their sins would need to be atoned for. And this truth was taught under the Old Testament form of worship, as it is described here, by the events which took place on the great Day of Atonement, where the high priest had a very special and important role to play.

2. The high priest changing his garments

Now we read here concerning holy garments which were made for Aaron. An important point about these garments is that Aaron could not enter into the presence of God without them. As long as he was without these garments, he was merely a private man, an ordinary Israelite. He could not enter the presence of God without these garments, or else he would die. If Aaron would presume to enter the presence of God without these garments, there was nothing for him but death. When his sons, Nadab and Abihu, entered into the presence of God presumptuously, with false fire, they were destroyed by fire from God. The fire of God's wrath met the fire of false incense and the fire of presumption. And even though they were the sons of Aaron and the nephews of Moses the man of God, that did not protect them. They were slain in the presence of God. This was a very solemn matter.

91

Now when Aaron entered the Holy Place, he wore these garments for glory and beauty. Bells and pomegranates hung on these garments, and as the priest went about his ministrations, the congregation were able to hear the bells sounding—and when they heard them, they rejoiced that they had a high priest in the presence of God. It was to them a joyful sound. They were a people who were blessed. How greatly blessed the people are, who know the joyful sound (Psalm 89:15), who understood that this joyful sound meant that the high priest was alive, and that he was carrying on his ministrations in the Holy Place.

But when we come to the Day of Atonement, there was a difference—a difference of the most significant nature. The robes for glory and beauty were laid aside. On the great Day of Atonement, when Aaron came before the Lord, he was there as the high priest and as the representative of Israel. He stood alone. No priest, no Levite, took any part in this event. Aaron stood alone. This was also said with regard to Christ, the divine High Priest—he was to tread the winepress alone. He said himself to his disciples that they would all forsake him and flee and leave him alone. There was no priest, there was no Levite, to take part in this great solemn event on the Day of Atonement in Israel, when the sins of Israel for that year were to be atoned for.

When Aaron laid aside the robes for glory and beauty on the Day of Atonement, he clothed himself instead in the holy garments of white linen, which were the garments of the ordinary priest. So when we come to the fulfilment of that Day of Atonement in the history of the Church of God, Christ the great High Priest laid aside his own garments of glory and beauty. When this type was fulfilled, the high priest was no longer of the house of Aaron, but a High Priest of the house of Judah, and after the order of Melchizedek. When he made atonement, it was for all the spiritual Israel of God, for all those sinners who were loved with an everlasting love, and who are to be drawn by the loving-kindness of God into fellowship with the God against whom they had sinned. When he came to this earth, the garments of glory and beauty were laid aside.

This teaches us about the humanity of Christ, the great High Priest. He came from the tribe of Judah, he was the Son of David, the root and the offspring of David, the bright and the morning star. (Aaron came from the tribe of Levi, but this High Priest came from the tribe of Judah, with regard to his human nature). Of course, the great High Priest came from the bosom of his Father, for he was and is and ever shall be the eternal Son of the everlasting Father, the Son of God, in truth and in love. Indeed, he came to be the High Priest of his people by the call of his everlasting Father. As Aaron here became the high priest by the call of God, so the New Testament Aaron became High Priest by the call of his everlasting Father. 'Thou art a priest for ever, after the order of Melchizedek.' This is the High Priest of our profession. What dishonour, and what trifling, to imagine that human priests are needed now that this priest has come! What a sham! What a colossal sham, to pretend that human priests are needed, when we have a high priest who is the Son of God, the eternal Son of the Father in truth and love!

Now there is a sense, of course, in which he was always clothed (with respect to his divine person) in glory and beauty. What beauty did he have? Well, he had this beauty: that he was the express image of the Father's person, and all the beauty of the Godhead was in the person of the Son. What glory did he have? He had this glory: that he was the out-shining of his Father's glory, the glory of God. That beauty and glory shone in him. These were the garments he wore in the bosom of his everlasting Father. And there was only one sense in which he could lay aside these garments. We must be particularly careful about this, and have a proper scriptural view of it. The Son of God could not lay aside the glory that belonged to him as God. He could not lay that aside. There is a theory, called the kenotic theory, much beloved by modern theologians, which says that Christ emptied himself of that glory. But that is not what the Scripture teaches, because he did not, and could not, lay aside these garments of glory and beauty—his own essential glory is eternal and unchangeable.

But he *did* lay aside his garments in this sense, that, just as Aaron clothed himself with the white linen garments of the ordinary priest, so this Priest, the Son of God, veiled his glory and beauty as God in the white linen garments of a holy humanity. His holy humanity was conceived by extraordinary or supernatural generation. I just wonder, from how many pulpits in Scotland, this doctrine will be taught when there's all this fuss and din about the birth of Christ. At any rate we know that the Bishop of Durham and others don't believe it. But the Scriptures teach that the humanity of Christ was conceived by the power of the Holy Ghost in the womb of Mary, and as the Son of God he took that humanity into union with his divine person, and so his glory and beauty as God was veiled as far as the eyes of men were concerned.

All of this was necessary for the Day of Atonement. All of this was necessary for *the* atonement. Because atoning for sin means this, that without the shedding of blood, there's no atoning for sin. The wages of sin is death. Death would have to be endured, the blood would have to be shed.

3. The high priest's actions on the Day of Atonement

On the Day of Atonement Aaron took the blood of bulls and of goats, which was shed for his own sins and for the sins of the people. Then he took the blood into the Holy Place. Before he did so, as we know, he took the censer and he took coals off the altar of incense (the golden altar just in front of the veil in the tabernacle) and he sprinkled the incense on the coal. A cloud of incense arose as he drew aside the curtain and went into the Most Holy Place, and rose up before the throne of God who dwelt between the cherubim. Then the high priest went back out, with the censer, and he closed the veil behind him. And then at this point, he took the blood of the sacrifice, which had been shed for the sins of Israel, and again he took aside the veil, again he went in to the Most Holy Place, and he sprinkled the blood seven times on the mercy seat and in front of the mercy seat. Now the sins of Israel were atoned for, for God saw the blood, and the blood atoned for sins. Then the high priest withdrew, and closed the veil again, and then he put on the garments for glory and beauty once more. When he put on these garments, and now began his service again, the golden bells were ringing, and the joyful sound was heard once more. Sin had been atoned for, and Israel was reconciled to God for that year.

So it was with our High Priest too. When he died on the cross of Calvary, he atoned for the sins of his people. His blood was shed for the remission of the sins of many. He drank the cup of death, so that his people could drink out of the cup of salvation. When he drank of the cup of death, there came a time when he cried on the cross, 'It is finished.' The cup of death was emptied. But the cup of salvation will never be empty. His people throughout the endless ages of eternity will be drinking out of this cup, and they'll *never* say it is finished.

So he died. At Calvary, the high priest was the sacrifice. There was neither bullock nor goat. He himself was the sacrifice. There was neither Levite nor priest. As in Israel's ceremony everything was done by the high priest alone, so it was with Jesus Christ. He died alone. And in his death alone there is the atoning sacrifice for sin.

His body was laid in the grave, the grave of Joseph of Arimathea. The body that came out of the virgin womb was now lying in a virgin tomb. What wonders! Lying in a tomb, where man never lay before. And when the time came, he rose again from the dead, by the power of an endless life. He ascended up on high. When he cried 'It is finished', the veil of the temple was rent in twain, from the top to the bottom, to show that the way into the presence of God was now open. And he who lay in the grave, he himself had said to his Father by the spirit of prophecy, 'Thou wilt show me the path of life.' The everlasting doors of heaven were opened, so that that this king and priest, this priestly king, might come into his own place, glorified in his holy humanity.

These are the garments of glory and beauty worn by our High Priest this Sabbath morning at God's right hand: his glorified humanity, and the glory of his divine person shining through that holy humanity, and filling heaven with that glory, the glory of God in Jesus Christ. We don't need priests in the New Testament era. We simply don't need them. Getting people to confess their sins, and giving them penances, getting them to say so many Hail Marys. We don't need that. An insufferable perversion of the truth! We have a High Priest in heaven, and if they had him, they would not be carrying on the way they are. We have our High Priest in heaven, and he is glorified in his holy humanity. These are his garments for glory and beauty. This High Priest entered, not the Holy Place made with hands, but into heaven itself, there to appear in the presence of God for us.

And when Christ entered in, he was bearing the merits of his death. God the Father said, 'Sit thou at my right hand' (Psalm 110:2). Now as the Mediator he was to share the throne of Jehovah, and be a Priest for ever at God's right hand. So if any man sin, we have an advocate with the Father, Jesus Christ the righteous and he is the propitiation for our sins (1 John 2:1, 2). He is a high priest for ever, after the order of Melchizedek. The holy garments were made for Aaron and his sons, and down through the generations that's what they were wearing. But that's all over and gone now—the special garments and the whole priesthood. It was all fulfilled when our glorious High Priest came, Jesus Christ, the eternal Son of the Father, the Melchizedek of the New Testament.

Now you remember what I said previously, that Aaron without these garments was just a private person, just like any other Israelite, as far as the worship of God was concerned. So this teaches us that Christ in his glorified humanity at God's right hand is not a private person, but he is there on behalf of his people. He is there as their High Priest in the presence of God.

4. The items worn by the high priest

Now we are told about various items that the priest wore. As I've been saying, we can understand the garments for glory and beauty as representing Christ's holy humanity glorified, glorified in such a way that the glory of his divine person can shine undiminished. (You see, when the glory of his divine person shone through his humanity on the Mount of Transfiguration, it was not undiminished, as Peter and James and John could not have stood the revelation of his undiminished glory. Indeed the glory that shone there was overwhelming to them, even in his humanity which had not then made the atoning sacrifice.) But now, at God's right hand, in his glorified humanity, he still has work to do on behalf of his people.

One item that the priest had to wear was the ephod. Part of the ephod fell down the front and part fell down the back. The two sides were clasped at the shoulder. And on the shoulder there were two precious stones—onyx stones, which had the names of the children of Israel engraved on them.

This meant that when Aaron went about his ministration, he was bearing on his shoulder the names of the twelve tribes of Israel. And what does that mean? It was intended to signify that in his person, *as the priest*, he was bearing them up, representing them, and acting for them. So it is with the Lord Jesus Christ. As the divine High Priest at God's right hand, he has on his shoulders (as it were) the names of his people, and he is there bearing them up in the presence of his Father. He secures for them that they will be borne up and that they will be carried through from the womb of the new birth to the Jordan of death, through the wilderness of time. Because of his work on their behalf, they will be carried through every trial, every temptation, every difficulty, and every burden until they cross the River Jordan into Immanuel's land. It occurs to me just now that we read also with regard to the Prince of Peace, that the government shall be upon his shoulders. 'Unto us a child is born, unto us a son is given, and the government shall be upon his shoulder, and his name shall be called Wonderful, Counsellor, the Mighty God, the Everlasting Father, the Prince of Peace.' He is governing for the people named on the two onyx stones. He is governing the world, he is governing providence, to preserve his people, and to see that not a hoof shall be left in Egypt. They shall all be brought, every one, with gladness great, and mirth on every side, into the palace of the King, and there they shall abide.

As it is described here, on the ephod there was also a breastplate, which was foursquare. On this breastplate there were also precious stones—in this case, twelve of them. These precious stones were set in four rows, three in each row. Engraved on these precious stones were the names of the twelve tribes of Israel, and this breastplate, we are told, was a memorial. That is to say, as the priest ministered in the Holy Place, he would have with him a memorial in the stones of the names of the twelve tribes of Israel. The high priest would carry this breastplate before the presence of God, and he would carry it upon his heart.

It is not immediately easy to understand why the two onyx stones were not enough, why there also had to be the breastplate and the twelve stones. Well, I believe it was for two reasons. First of all, because it indicates that our

97

glorious high priest at God's right hand not only carries all his people on his shoulders to support them, but he carries them on his heart because he loves them. And since he has them on his heart, they are continually before the eye of his Father, for the Father loves them also. The other reason seems to be that whereas the onyx stones were two stones, on the twelve stones there is what we might call a more particular numbering of the people. This emphasises the fact that when Christ bears his people on his heart before the throne of his Father, he does not bear them as it were in the mass, but he bears them as though they were single, as though each one was there individually enjoying the fullness of his love and the fullness of his care. There is a particularity about Christ's intercession.

Many of the people of God may feel doubts about this great matter, whether they are in the breastplate of the High Priest. Oh, they can believe that Aaron was there, they can believe that Moses was there, they can believe that Jeremiah is there, they can believe that Paul and Silas are there, they can believe that the people of God whom they knew in the world, whose fellowship they enjoyed, were there—but what about themselves? Well, the twelve stones on the breastplate emphasise the particularity of Christ's work, that is, that Christ bears every one of them—every one of them!—before his heart, as a memorial before God. Can they ever be forgotten? How could they be! The mountains shall depart, and the hills may be removed, but they will never be forgotten. They are before the throne of God in the heart of the High Priest, as a memorial. They can never be forgotten. There may be turbulences in the world, as there are even now over the Gulf War. But those who are among the tribes of the spiritual Israel, they're all on the breastplate, they're all in the heart of the High Priest, and they're all borne in love before the throne of the everlasting Father. As I was saying last Sabbath, he prays for them specially: 'I pray for them: I pray not for the world' (John 17:9).

The world think the people of God are to be despised. They cannot join in all the jollification and all the office parties. Very strange! I was in an office myself in my younger days and although at normal times, in normal working relations, there was an atmosphere of friendliness, then you came to this time, Christmas time and the office party. When you didn't go, you could feel the deep resentment. I've often mentioned it, although perhaps not so much in public, one of the darkest days that I spent during the five years that I was in the Navy in the War was down in Campbeltown, on a Christmas day, when I refused to have anything to do with the frivolities and the carnal enjoyments that went on among the officers and the rest. And I remember so well the feeling of enmity against this. Let that be as it is: God's people are on the breastplate of the High Priest. In heaven. That's where they're going to be eventually, because he is there. 'Where I am, there ye may be also' is what he pleads for them in his intercession.

We also see that the breastplate is called the breastplate of judgment. That was because of the Urim and the Thummim. Now these are rather mysterious terms. But it would be sufficient to say this, that when Aaron made use of the Urim and Thummim in consulting God, he received light on the case of Israel. The same, we may say, is true with Christ: in his intercession, he obtains judgment for his people. Even in this world, he obtains and gives light upon their case. Of course, he will also eventually obtain judgment for his people at the Day of Judgment, when they shall be delivered from all the accusations made against them.

The other item that is mentioned here is the mitre with a gold plate. On the mitre was inscribed 'Holiness to the Lord'. It was necessary for the high priest to wear this mitre, or crown. I believe the reason is similar to the situation that we are familiar with from British history, namely that whatever the monarch used to do in his official capacity, like signing a bill, he wore the royal crown, and then the signature made that bill an Act of Parliament because all the dignity of the British Crown was behind his signature. So this mitre, 'Holiness to the Lord', summarises all the dignity of the priest's work. The attribute of holiness shines through all that belonged to the high priest. The Lord our God is holy still. The High Priest is holy. He wears the crown of holiness. His glory and his beauty are bound up with the out-shining of *holiness*. And all the people who will be gathered there will be perfect in holiness.

Let us now look further at the garments. As it says here, round the rim of the robe at the bottom there was a pomegranate and a golden bell, a pomegranate and a golden bell alternating round the hem of his garment. The pomegranate points to the fruit of the atonement. In our case, it reminds us of the fruit of the death of our High Priest. Part of his glory is that his people are saved in him. Does he not say so? 'They shall be mine,' saith the Lord of hosts, 'in that day when I make up my jewels' (Malachi 3:17). Part of his glory is to have them as his people—this is part of the glory that will shine in heaven when he will present them before the Father and say, 'Behold I and the children which thou hast given me.' They will be there without spot and without blemish, glorified in their own humanity, glorified in bearing in their souls and bodies the image of the first-begotten from the dead, the Lord and Saviour Jesus Christ. The pomegranates point to the fruit of Christ's death, the eternal salvation of his people.

The golden bells tell us how this fruit is to be gathered in—Christ's people are saved with a joyful sound. Remember that after the atonement had been made, the high priest put on the garments for glory and beauty, and as he now went about his ministrations, the people were able to hear the bells. This was the joyful sound that they heard—Aaron is alive: he did not die! Unlike Nadab and Abihu, his offering was accepted. So the joyful sound of the everlasting gospel is a testimony to the fact that our High Priest is in heaven. When the joyful sound of the preaching of the gospel is so despised in our day and generation, it can only be because people don't know this High Priest, and don't understand his work. But one of the evidences that Christ is at God's right hand was the outpouring of the Holy Spirit on the day of Pentecost. On that day, three thousand souls heard the bells ring. Yes, there they heard the joyful sound, the golden bells telling of the success of the high priest's work. They began to say, 'God's mercies I will ever sing' (Psalm 89:1). They began to sing, 'O greatly blessed the people are / the joyful sound that know' (Psalm 89:15)—the joyful sound that Christ died for the ungodly, that he is risen again, that he is now at God's right hand, a Prince and a Saviour to give repentance and forgiveness of sins (Acts 5:31).

100

Others may despise the gospel. Ordinary people and even professors of theology may despise the gospel. But that is because they don't see the glory of it, they don't know the joyful sound themselves. They may despise it, they may turn their back on it, they may say the gospel era is now over, and we must get something new now. But no. It's not over. Of course many among those who love the gospel have their fears and doubts. We're afraid that ministers are dying out. We're afraid that ministers aren't being raised up. We're afraid of this and we're afraid of that. But what I have to say to you is: as long as the High Priest is at God's right hand, the gospel will be preached. I don't say it will always be preached in Glasgow, or even in Scotland, but it will be preached somewhere in the world, somewhere where there are sinners to be gathered in to Christ. There's no doubt about it. By the preaching of the gospel, the fruit is to be gathered in. By the gospel they shall be brought out of darkness into his marvellous light. 'He out of darkness did them bring, / and from death's shade them take; / these bands, wherewith they had been bound, / asunder quite he brake' (Psalm 107:14). And so the ransomed of the Lord shall return to Zion, with songs and everlasting joy upon their heads, and for them, sorrow and sighing shall flee away (Isaiah 35:10).

5. The anointing of the high priest

Now the last thing I'm going to mention is that the garments for glory and beauty were anointed with the holy oil, and so was Aaron himself. You remember that this is mentioned in Psalm 133 (we'll sing that at the end of the service): 'Like precious ointment on the head, / that down the beard did flow, ev'n Aaron's beard, and to the skirts / did of his garments go.' Christ our High Priest is anointed with the Holy Spirit without measure, in order that sinners might hear the joyful sound—in order that they might rejoice in the Lord—in order that they might rejoice in his salvation. This comes about through the gracious work of the Holy Ghost, convincing of sin and misery, enlightening the mind in the knowledge of Christ, renewing the will, persuading and enabling the soul to embrace Christ, as he is freely offered in the everlasting gospel. They embrace him, to have him as their salvation, and to love him. 'Whom having not seen, ye love', and now 'believing, ye rejoice with joy unspeakable and full of glory' (1 Peter 1:8). They rejoice, believing in Christ who is revealed in the Word of God—believing that he is now at God's right hand—believing that he is now clothed in the garments for glory and for beauty—believing that he is there for his people, not as a private person but as a public person, as a priest for his people. All his people are in him, they are upon his breastplate, they are upon his shoulders. How safe they are! Why should they be discouraged? Why should they be cast down, when they have such a glorious High Priest?

He is anointed with the oil of joy above his fellows. I believe that that is one of the things that makes the Lord's people rejoice in their hearts—the thought that the Lord Jesus Christ who suffered such pain and sorrow and desolation on the cross of Calvary is now anointed with the oil of joy. He himself is enjoying the pleasures that are at God's right hand for ever more. But, as I said already and I hope I've made it clear, the pomegranates are there too, the fruits—his people are all there. In the Old Testament ceremonies, the children of Israel remained in the outer court—the Levites too remained in the outer court—the priests themselves could not go any nearer than the Holy Place. But in heaven there are no courts. It's all one temple, without any divisions, and the whole family are around the throne of God. Their High Priest and their elder brother is there with them—he is anointed with the oil of joy, and it's flowing down to his fellows. He was anointed with the oil of joy above his fellows, but the oil of joy is also flowing down into their souls, and that is what's happening moment by moment (if we can use the words) throughout the eternal ages.

That is prospect of the Lord's people. When they get that joy in their souls, it is the first moment of their entering everlasting glory where they see Christ, and this joy distils in their souls. One drop of this joy will be enough to dispel all that they suffered in this world for Christ and for his sake. That joy is joy that will never come to an end, because the High Priest is the High Priest for ever.

May he bless his Word. Let us call upon his name.

Eternal and ever blessed one, do thou graciously bless thy Word to us, and give us grace to rejoice that Christ is now in everlasting glory, that he is at thy right hand, that he is clothed in the garments of glory and beauty, the garments of a glorified humanity, and that thy glory is in him, shining in everlasting glory, and that thy people are rejoicing in it. Do thou be gracious to each one of us here, and grant that we might have the prayer of Moses the man of God when he prayed, 'Show me thy glory', that we might be followers of Christ through good and evil report. Give us grace now to sing to thy praise. Pardon our many sins for Christ's sake. Amen.

6 Christ the King

ACTS 17:7

There is another king, one Jesus.

Lord's Day evening, 23rd December 1990

Those of you who were here this morning will recollect that I was drawing the attention of the congregation to the great High Priest, this Jesus Christ, the High Priest of our profession. We were considering the glory and the dignity that belongs to him, as he is now exalted at God's right hand, the High Priest in the court of heaven. 'If any man sin, we have an advocate with the Father, Jesus Christ the righteous' (1 John 2:1).

On this occasion I desire to bring before you the teaching of the Word of God that the same person who is the great High Priest is also the King. Christ is the Mediator who has been appointed between God and man, and in his mediatorial office, he is revealed as Prophet, Priest and King. The Word of God not only includes the doctrine of the Priesthood of Christ but also the doctrine of his Kingship. Christ is King. He is the King appointed by God the Father, and he is the King who is preached in the gospel of the glory of the blessed God. Therefore we find Paul and others preaching the truth that there is another king as well as Caesar.

Now it will hardly be necessary for me to say that in teaching this doctrine the apostle was not guilty of sedition, as he was accused of here. Jesus is King of a spiritual kingdom. His kingdom is not like the kingdom of the Caesars, a kingdom that belongs to this world, and a kingdom that will perish with this world. His is a kingdom that is spiritual and therefore eternal. His kingdom will have no end at all. Therefore this flimsy accusation of supposed sedition falls to the ground. It was worthless, baseless and vain, because proclaiming the kingship of Christ does not undermine the lawful authority of secular rulers to rule.

Now when these men took Jason and the other brethren before the authorities, they complained that when the apostles taught that there was another king as well as Caesar, they were going contrary to the decrees of Caesar. According to the decrees passed in Caesar's worldly kingdom, nobody was supposed to mention another king within the Roman empire, within the rule and sovereignty of Caesar. But the apostles were acting in obedience to another decree—not the decree of Caesar, but the decree of God himself. That is why we sang Psalm 2, because there we are told that this King will 'declare the decree'—a decree which supersedes the commandments and regulations of all earthly authorities.

1. In the first place, then, we shall consider the decree of God—not the decrees of Caesar, which only had a limited range when they were in force, and which have no existence now at all—but the decree of God. The decrees of God are the purposes of God which he conceived in eternity and brings to pass in time. The purposes and counsels of men come to an end: 'O but the counsel of the Lord / doth stand for ever sure; / and of his heart the purposes / from age to age endure' (Psalm 33:11).

2. Secondly we shall consider that this King has ambassadors. That in fact was the work of Paul and the other apostles, as Paul himself declared: 'We are ambassadors for Christ' (2 Corinthians 5:20). Caesar had his decrees— 'Conquer by the power of the sword!' But this King conquers by the power of the sceptre of the Word of God, which liveth and abideth for ever. Of course, King Jesus is now in heaven, where he can only be seen with the eye of faith, but in every age and generation since his ascension to heaven, he sends out his ambassadors to speak on his behalf.

3. On behalf of this King, the ambassadors declare the peace of God to the children of men. On his behalf, his ambassadors call on sinners of the human race to 'kiss the Son', to be reconciled to this King, 'lest in his ire, ye perish from the way', for blessed are those who trust in him, who believe in him, who receive him, who come to be at peace with God through him.

1. The decree of God

Because of the great extent of the Roman Empire—which ruled over large stretches of the world—the decrees of Caesar were important for those who lived in his empire. They were supposed to demonstrate his glory, and the glory of his kingdom. But when Caesar died, his decrees died too. Caesar's decrees were authoritative only for as long as he was ruling. By contrast, the decree which we are considering is authoritative for ever. It takes to do with the glory of the God who created the ends of the earth. It will stand for ever, and it demonstrates the glory of God himself.

The first thing we shall consider in this decree is that it makes reference to a king. 'I have set my King upon my holy hill of Zion.' Yes, Christ is the King of the Church. Yes, Christ is King of kings and Lord of lords. But notice here that God the Father is speaking, and he calls him 'my King'. He is the Father's King. In the decree of God, in the purposes of the heart of God, Christ was set aside to be his King. King Jesus is God's king.

Now, God being an eternal being, the decree of God was formed in eternity. It takes place in time—all God's decrees take place in time—but the decree itself is eternal, it is the purpose of the everlasting God.

The purpose of the everlasting God in this decree is that he would set his King on the holy hill of Zion. By God's authority and God's decree, Jesus is set as King on the holy hill of Zion. That is to say, his kingship is revealed in connection with the Church of God in the world. God's holy hill of Zion was the place where God was worshipped in this world, where his people gathered together to worship him. This King was set up and revealed in the Church of the living God. So we see that the decree of God embraces God's purpose with regard to his Church. This decree teaches us that included in

God's decree was a purpose to deliver a number that no man can number of the human family: he purposed to deliver them from being the servants of sin and Satan, and to deliver them to be the children of God. In setting this King upon Zion his holy hill, God's purpose was that many sons would be brought to glory (Hebrews 2:10). They would be brought to Zion in this world, and they would eventually be brought to the Zion above.

This decree also describes the people who are to be brought in. We see from Psalm 2 that the King is to ask of God, and God will give him the heathen for his inheritance, and the uttermost parts of the earth for his possession. These are the many sons who are to be brought to glory. The heathen were without God and without hope in the world. They were sinners of mankind, alienated from the life of godliness through the hardness of their heart. They were sinners by nature and sinners by practice, enemies to God by wicked works. And yet this King was to have them as his possession! He would ask for them, and he would receive them as his possession. And he would have them to the uttermost parts of the earth—not only within the bounds of Israel, but among the Gentiles and to the ends of the earth. Caesar had a great empire, one of the greatest empires the world ever saw. But this King is promised a more glorious empire still. This was prophesied away back in the days of Jacob. When he was on his death bed, Jacob was given the spirit of prophecy, and when speaking of the tribe of Judah you remember he said, 'The sceptre shall not depart from Judah, nor a lawgiver from between his feet, until Shiloh come; and unto him shall the gathering of the people be' (Genesis 49:10). Shiloh is another name for the Prince of Peace, the King of Zion, God's King, and the Hebrew word for 'people' there refers to the Gentiles.

So even in the days of Jacob the prophecy was declared, the decree was unfolded: it was made known that this King would have the uttermost parts of the earth for his possession. Every other empire that ever was, it rose and it fell. The empire of Egypt rose and fell—the empires of Persia—Babylon—Greece—Rome—they rose, they fell. Yes, and sad to say, even the empire of Britain. But this is a kingdom that has no end at all, and will remain. This

King will remain and will rule by the sceptre of his Word over this kingdom, while sun and moon endure. The enemies of Christ in this world, in this generation, are fond of saying that the kingdom of Christ is over—the time for the gospel is over. The generation that has discovered how to land on the moon, the generation that has made all manner of technological advances— they are not going to listen to a message about a King who they cannot see and a kingdom which they cannot examine with their scientific instruments. But their trust in science and technology is a delusion. Christ's kingdom has no end at all. It has its times when it is small, compared to former days—at least in certain places—but let us not be discouraged. The King still reigns, and he will have his possession.

Now we also find in the decree this statement: 'The Lord hath said to me, / Thou art mine only Son; this day / I have begotten thee.' When we read, 'the Lord has said unto me', this is as much as to say, 'the Father says to the Son'. This brings before us the eternal communion between the Father and the Son. The eternal communion between God the Father and God the Son in the communion of the Holy Ghost. Now we must be careful here. While this communion takes place with regard to the decree, the generation of the Son is not part of the decree. The Son is the only begotten of the Father, but God the Father did not decree that he would have a Son. Now that's important because this is the *eternal* Son. The generation of the Son was a necessary act on the part of the Father, part of the glory of the Father's person. So when we are speaking of the decree, although it is eternal, and the Father and the Son have communion with regard to it, the person of the Son is not the *result* of the divine decree. The results of the divine decree happen in time, but the Son is the Son eternally. I just mention this in passing. These are great subjects, worthy of meditation, worthy of a human soul to meditate on.

But in this communion we see what the decree reveals. According to the declaration of the decree, the person who is God's King is God's Son. The person who is God's King is none less than God's Son. 'This day,' he says, 'I have begotten thee.' The generation of the Son, the begetting of the Son, is an eternal act. This day is a day that had no morning—it is a day upon which the shades of night will never fall. It is the day of eternity, without beginning, without end. Eternally God had and possessed his beloved Son, and now, in the decree for the purposes to be carried out in time, this was God's King, appointed and instituted by God. God's King is God the eternal Son, and he is constituted to be God's King, the King over God's kingdom.

If the domains of Caesar took their glory from the presence of Caesar on the throne in Rome, then surely the glory of this kingdom is derived from the glory of its King. The eternal Son of the eternal Father, God in the second person, is the King on Zion, God's holy hill. This King can never be overthrown—all the powers of the world cannot overthrow him—and his kingdom, the Church, can never be overthrown: it is built on the Rock of the eternal person of the divine Redeemer, Jesus the Son of God. 'We believe and are sure that thou art that Christ, the Son of the living God' (John 6:69) and therefore the gates of hell, all the counsels of hell, shall never prevail against it.

Here we have 'another King, one Jesus'. In Thessalonica and in Philippi, this is who they were proclaiming. This was part of the unfolding of the decree. In the decree, the Son of God was to become the Son of man. The King was one called Jesus, Jesus Christ the Messiah. Even over his cross they wrote the words 'Jesus, the King of the Jews.' The soldiers mocked him, they put a crown and a robe on him, they jeeringly said, 'Hail, King of the Jews!'—but they did not know that the person who they mocked was God's King and God's Son.

So this King has this name: not only is he the Son of God, but he is called Jesus, for he shall save his people from their sins. He is a King who is a Saviour—a Saviour from sin—and in order that he might be so, he became man. According to God's prophecy he was born in Bethlehem. Now you know that at Christmas time, this city of Glasgow, like Athens in Paul's time, is given to idolatry. All the decorations and the tinsel: worthless! Christmas has nothing whatever to do with Christianity: nothing whatever! It's much more connected with Popery, not with Christianity. But you see it suits the people of our generation to speak about this king as little more than a child that they can make a model of—they can put it in a cradle and they can move it about here, there and anywhere according to their will. But in reality, this King who became the Son of man is the Son of God, and he became the Son of man in order to save sinners from their sins. And as you all know, he became man through the supernatural work of the Holy Spirit in the womb of Mary, conceiving there a holy, pure, human nature. The Son of God took that human nature into union with his divine person. He was born into this world, as the King whose name is called Jesus, for he shall save his people from their sins. That was a fulfilment of the decree of God. God decreed it from eternity. He told it, he declared the decree by the Spirit of prophecy, and it was fulfilled.

2. The King's ambassadors

Now here are the ambassadors of this King. And what are they doing when they're talking about this King? They are speaking about this King *as he is revealed in the Scriptures*. They do not speak of him as he comes into their own imagination, but as he is the King who is revealed and made known in the Scriptures.

Paul 'opened and alleged' *from the Scriptures* certain things with regard to this king. That is to say, he opened the Scriptures, giving an exposition of the Scripture, alleging that what the Scripture said was true, namely, that 'this Jesus, whom I preach unto you, is Christ', the King.

The King who sends the ambassadors

Now what about this King, this King of glory, this glorious one in the nature of man? What is the Scripture telling us? How was the decree fulfilled with regard to him? Paul expounds several things that were absolutely necessary in order for this King to be this Saviour.

He suffered. Indeed, he 'must needs have suffered' (Acts 17:3). This is a suffering King, and there was a need for the suffering. He was persecuted, he was mocked, he was ultimately crucified. Men carried out that evil work. The Jewish nation are suffering to the present day on account of that. And note in passing that the attempt to make out that such a statement is anti-Semitic is just an idea that is absurd, because when we say this, we look forward to the future conversion of the Jews, for 'what shall the receiving of them be, but life from the dead?' (Romans 11:15). There is no contradiction between acknowledging that the Jews have been cut off for unbelief and asserting with Paul that 'they are beloved for the fathers' sakes'. The Jews said with regard to this King, 'His blood be on us, and on our children' (Matthew 27:25). Until they come to acknowledge that Jesus is the Messiah, they must lie under that.

He suffered. He drank the cup of death—the cup which was filled with the sins of his people, and the death that was due to all these sins. That cup was so great that no-one could take it up and put it to the mouth of Jesus Christ but God the everlasting Father. There was not an angel in glory who could take hold of that cup and lift it up for him to drink, nor all the angels in glory together: they would have disappeared down into the blackness of darkness forever. That is why this King called it 'the cup which my Father hath given me'—it is given by my Father who appointed me King. And he says, 'Shall I not drink it?' In his sufferings unto death, in his being crucified on the cross, he made an end of that cup, crying on the cross, 'It is finished.' That death which was eternal came to an end in time, because the person who drank it in his holy humanity was a divine, eternal, infinite, unchangeable person. By this death, this King has bruised the head of the serpent, the head of the god of this world. And Satan knows that this King will take to himself those who are in the kingdom of darkness, in his own time.

He must needs have suffered. The need for his sufferings was the need to satisfy the inflexible, holy justice of God, which required that the death due to these sins would be endured either in the person of the sinner or in the person of the Saviour. According to the decree of God, it was endured on the cross of Calvary in the person of the Saviour. It was the King that died. What a wonder! Was there ever such a wonderful King, who died so that his people might be saved, and who manifested in his death his love to them, his love to each one of them? Paul could say, 'The life which I now live, … I live by the faith of the Son of God, who loved me, and gave himself for me' (Galatians 2:20).

But not only was there a need for him to suffer, he must also rise from the dead (verse 3). There was a need for his resurrection too. That was needed in order to display and make known that this King had finished the cup of death, and to display and make known that this King had conquered the king of terrors. People don't like to think that death is the king of terrors—they prefer to think that death is just the human cycle coming to an end, there's no afterlife, no judgment, no eternity—and especially, no eternal death. But death *is* the king of terrors, to those who die in their sins, and this King has overcome it. He has conquered death and the grave, as he said long ago by the prophet Hosea, long before the cross of Calvary, and long before the resurrection morning. 'O death, I will be thy plagues; O grave, I will be thy destruction' (Hosea 13:14). When he rose (by the power of an endless life) he rose as a conqueror over death and the grave.

He rose, also, to assure all his people that they too will rise on the morning of the resurrection, when time shall be no longer. 'I am the resurrection, and the life: he that believeth in me, though he were dead, yet shall he live: and whosoever liveth and believeth in me shall never die' (John 11:25, 26)—he shall have eternal life.

This is the Saviour! This is the Saviour—the risen Lord, the one who ascended up on high, the one for whom the everlasting doors were opened, in order that the King of glory would come into his place at God's right hand. And when he came into his place, God the Father set upon his head the crown of purest gold—the crown of a glorified Saviour is now on the head of Jesus. The head that wore the crown of thorns is now wearing the crown of purest gold. Let us never forget that on his coronation day, when God the Father set upon his head a crown of purest gold, and declared to him that he would have all that his heart desired, he would never have worn a crown of gold if he had not first worn the crown of thorns. The crown of gold would never have gone on the head of the glorified humanity of Christ if the crown of thorns had not first pierced that humanity.

So this is our glorious King! And the Caesars, and the Gorbachevs with their Nobel Prizes, and all the rest of them, they can make a great fuss here in the world, and there can be revolutions, and wars, and rumours of wars (and our King has told us not to be surprised, for these things must be)—but this King is above it all. He is above and beyond it all. He is now at God's right hand, a Prince and a Saviour. We have another King, and altogether another kingdom than the kingdoms of this world and the kingdom of darkness.

The work of the King's ambassadors
So let us consider further the work of the ambassadors of this King. Now, it's a mark of all his ambassadors that when they preach about this King, they preach from the Scriptures. Why? Because they believe that in the Scriptures you have a revelation of the decree of God and how it is carried out in time—they believe that the Scriptures are the Word of God, infallible, inerrant, inspired by the third person of the Godhead. If some people do not believe that, they may call themselves ambassadors, and others may call them ambassadors, but they have neither part nor lot with the King: Christ never sent them. It is so obvious that the ambassadors must preach from the Word of God, because all the ambassadors of this King know him as their own Saviour. They did not garner their knowledge of the King from the Scriptures in a merely intellectual way—rather, they came to the knowledge of this King in their spiritual experience. They are preaching a King who is unseen, a King at God's right hand, but he is a King who they have come to know spiritually, experimentally, in their own experience, through the operation of the Spirit of God in effectual calling. They were born again, and they came to know Christ and the power of his resurrection. Because they came to know Christ as the Saviour of their own souls, therefore when they speak of him, they speak of him as one who they know, one they have communion and fellowship with, one who is precious to them. Unto you that believe, Christ is precious. Their minds need to have been enlightened in the knowledge of the glory of this King before they are called to be ambassadors and sent forth to be ambassadors for him.

They are sent out to be ambassadors for this King who is now exalted to God's right hand. He is the King of whom we were singing in Psalm 2: 'Ask of me, and for heritage / the heathen I'll make thine; / And, for possession, I to thee / will give earth's utmost line.' Now that this King is exalted to God's right hand, he is coming into possession of his people. So we sang also in Psalm 21 these words, 'He asked life of thee, and thou gavest it him, even length of days for ever and ever. His glory is great in thy salvation: honour and majesty hast thou laid upon him.' So the sending forth of the ambassadors is bound up with God the Father saying to this King, 'Ask of me, and for heritage / the heathen I'll make thine.' Christ is to have this possession, not by the sword, not by atomic bombs, but by the sceptre of the Word of God, through the ambassadors that he sends forth.

So here they are in Europe. Paul was going to Asia and the Holy Ghost forbade him. He was not to go at that time. He was to go to Asia later (and he did—there were seven churches in Asia, which we read about in the book of Revelation), but for now he was in Europe—the gospel was on its way to Britain, on its way to Glasgow. As the ambassador of Christ, Paul was declaring and preaching that there is another King, other than Caesar. He was warning them with regard to this world, with regard to the glories of the kingdoms of this world, with regard to the reign and rule of the god of this world, that old serpent the devil and Satan. There is another King! Paul was calling to sinners in the gospel to be reconciled to God through this King— to be reconciled to God through the death that he died, through the blood that was shed in that death which was for the remission of the sins of many (Matthew 26:28).

Opening and alleging. That's the work of the ambassadors—it's to open up the Word of God, to explain it in its own light and by the grace of the Holy Spirit. There is another King, one Jesus! The ambassadors address the children of men, first of all warning them there is another King—warning them that they have needs other than the needs of this world. Caesar may and does to some extent provide for the needs of the body, but the kingdoms of this world cannot provide for the needs of the soul. There is only one king who can do that, only one king who can prepare your soul for death, for judgment and for eternity, and that is King Jesus. Therefore the ambassadors preach the gospel of the glory of the blessed God. We then, as ambassadors for Christ, we pray you in Christ's stead—in the stead of this King, we pray you, be reconciled to God!

How are you to be reconciled to God? You are to be reconciled to the King. 'Kiss ye the Son!'—be reconciled through the King to God the Father. What does it mean to 'kiss the King'? Well, it means this first of all, that your soul becomes reconciled to the fact that without this King you are lost. Without this King you are a child of hell, you are a child of wrath. Without this King you will perish eternally. And the second thing is that you see and understand that in this King there is eternal salvation for the very chief of sinners, and you are reconciled to receiving this salvation, without money and without price. You are reconciled to the fact that it is a salvation which can never be obtained by human works or endeavours, but you welcome Christ. The kiss is a kiss of welcome. That's what faith is—it is a welcoming of Christ, it is an embracing of Christ, it is embracing the King to be your Saviour, and resting in him and in his salvation as all your salvation and all your desire. 'Kiss ye the Son!'

3. The declaration of Christ's ambassadors

I must go on now to speak about the last thing. This king is the Prince of Peace, and in the gospel he is freely offering peace to sinners. Peace with God through the Lord Jesus Christ. He himself preaches peace through the blood of his cross, by his ambassadors.

Peace and reconciliation are held out to us in the gospel, and sinners are invited to receive it. But what of those who refuse the invitation? The alternative is clear. 'Kiss the Son, lest he be angry, and ye perish from the way, when his wrath is kindled but a little.' He is invisible now but there's a day coming—it's on the wing—it's in the decree of God—and this King will be visible. Every eye that sees me this Sabbath evening standing in this pulpit here is destined by the decree of God to see Christ. We read about this towards the end of this chapter: 'he hath appointed a day' (Acts 17:31). There you are! There's the decree! He has appointed a day in which he will judge the world in righteousness, by that man who he has ordained, and he has given assurance of this to all men, in that he has raised him from the dead.

This King will appear on the day of judgment. He will be visible on the great white throne, and the dead, small and great, will stand before him, and also those who pierced him. Small and great, they will see this King in his glory, in the glory of his Father and the glory of the holy angels. And the books will be opened, and you will be there, and I will be there, and just as surely as you and I see one another this evening, it is appointed that you and I will see Christ on the great white throne. The dead will be brought from their graves, and they will stand before that throne. This King will pass judgment. He will separate for eternity the sheep and the goats. The father from his children, the husband from his wife, the wife from her husband. Those who came to kiss the Son are the sheep of Christ, and those who refused to kiss the Son, they are the goats. The King will say to his own people, 'Come, ye blessed of my Father, inherit the kingdom prepared for you from the foundation of the world.' They were in the kingdom of grace in this world, but now they are invited into the kingdom of glory. To the others, those on his left hand, he will say, 'Depart from me, ye cursed, into everlasting fire, prepared for the devil and his angels.' What sad and terrible words, 'prepared for the devil and his angels'! But now multitudes of the children of men, by their refusal to acknowledge Zion's King, are there for ever and ever.

Now consider lastly that this King has a worldwide conquest. Among those who will be gathered at his right hand there will be some from every nation and kindred and tribe and tongue. That will be seen on the day of judgment. The ends of the earth were given to him for a possession and he will secure their salvation. You and I may not see it taking place in time, but surely we can believe by faith the decree of God revealed in his Word, that Christ will have the ends of the earth for his inheritance. Our King is to have this glory, that all ends of the earth will turn to him. 'All ends of the earth remember shall, / and turn the Lord unto; / All kindreds of the nations / to him shall homage do' (Psalm 22:27). These days are yet to be seen on this earth which is now laden with sin and iniquity, but they will come before this world passes away—days of glory, days when the King of Zion will use the sceptre of his Word, by the power of his Holy Ghost, to gather innumerable souls to taste and see that God is good and who trusts in him is blessed.

Now this is your day and mine. What we are to listen to this day is this: 'Kiss ye the Son, lest in his ire / ye perish from the way, / If once his wrath begin to burn: / blessed all that on him stay.' Blessed, blessed are those who depend on him, who believe on him, who trust in him! They shall never be put to shame.

May he bless his Word. Let us call upon his name.

7 Christk the Prophet

DEUTERONOMY 18:15-18

The Lord thy God will raise up unto thee a Prophet from the midst of thee, of thy brethren, like unto me; unto him ye shall hearken; according to all that thou desiredst of the Lord thy God in Horeb in the day of the assembly, saying, Let me not hear again the voice of the Lord my God, neither let me see this great fire any more, that I die not. And the Lord said unto me, They have well spoken that which they have spoken. I will raise them up a Prophet from among their brethren, like unto thee, and will put my words in his mouth; and he shall speak unto them all that I shall command him.

LORD'S DAY MORNING, 30TH DECEMBER 1990

Last Sabbath morning we endeavoured to deal with the priestly office of the Lord and Saviour Jesus Christ, and in the evening we endeavoured to deal with the kingly office of the same divine and glorious Redeemer. I therefore thought it appropriate that this Sabbath morning we should deal with the third office or function of the Mediator, and that is his prophetic office. These are the three functions or offices of the one Mediator, the only Mediator between God and man, the Lord Jesus Christ. He is the Prophet, the Priest and the King of his Church.

In these verses from Deuteronomy we have the God of Abraham, Isaac and Jacob, the God of salvation, giving this promise in the days of Moses to the Church of God, namely that he would raise up to the Church a Prophet from the midst of the brethren, someone like unto Moses.

This promise was given when the Church of God was in the wilderness, and it was fulfilled one thousand five hundred years later, when the Church was entering into the new testament dispensation, leaving the wilderness, and entering into a settled state, concerning which the Word of God says, we have received a kingdom which cannot be moved (Hebrews 12:28). The Church in the wilderness moved from time to time, according to the movements of the pillar of cloud by day and the pillar of fire by night, but we are now in a kingdom which cannot be moved. We have come to a state, a dispensation, that is final as far as the Church in this world is concerned.

This promise was fulfilled fifteen hundred years after it was given. We find Peter telling the people in the Book of Acts, 'Moses truly said unto the fathers, A prophet shall the Lord your God raise up unto you of your brethren, like unto me; him shall ye hear in all things whatsoever he shall say unto you. And it shall come to pass, that every soul' (mark you, *every* soul) 'which will not hear that prophet, shall be destroyed from among the people' (Acts 3:32).

One day with the Lord is as a thousand years, and a thousand years as one day. We must remember that he has his own time for fulfilling his promises. He had his own time for fulfilling *this* promise—the Church had to wait all these years for it to be fulfilled—but fulfilled it was. Every other promise will also be fulfilled, however long it may take. We should remember this. We should not be discouraged by the length of time that the promise takes to be fulfilled—it will be fulfilled in God's good time. It may be a long time to wait before all ends of the earth shall remember and turn to the Lord. These very ends of the earth that are now forgetting God and his Christ will yet remember and turn to the Lord, and all kindreds of the nations shall do homage to this Prophet, to this Priest and to this King. Let us then be determined to be assured that we will be among those in this generation who will do homage to him.

1. Now we shall consider first of all the need there was for a Prophet—and the need there still is. For although this Prophet is now in heaven, he still exercises his prophetic office there. You remember that Christ exercises

his offices of Prophet, Priest and King both in a state of humiliation and in a state of glorification. Moses was a great prophet, but Moses' days came to an end, and the Lord buried him in the hills of Moab. Unlike Moses, the Prophet we have now, the one who was raised up like unto Moses, is still alive, and alive for evermore, and what is more, he is exercising his prophetic office in his state of glory. (I say his prophetic office, although I prefer the word 'function', because it keeps in view that the mediatorial office is one. The mediatorial office, which is one, has these three functions, of Prophet, Priest and King.)

2. Then secondly we shall enquire as to who this Prophet is. Here we see a most remarkable thing. This Prophet is to be raised up like unto Moses, who, we are told, was faithful in all the house of God as a servant. But the Prophet that we are to speak of is a Son. He is a Son over his house, and yet at the same time, we are told here that he is to be raised up from among the brethren. That Prophet is the Lord and Saviour Jesus Christ.

3. Then we shall consider how he exercised and continues to exercise his prophetic office.

1. The need for a prophet

First of all, the need that we have of a prophet. This need arises from the same basic need that we have of a Mediator between us and God, although each of the mediatorial functions deals with a different aspect of our need.

As we were indicating last Sabbath morning, we need to have a Mediator who is a priest. On account of our sins, we have separated ourselves from God, and we are unable to reconcile ourselves to the God against whom we have sinned—not by any endeavours of our own, of any description or kind. We need a priest, so that through his sacrifice our guilt may be taken away, and so that through his blood we may be reconciled to God. 'Through his blood, ye who were sometimes afar off are now made nigh.' Made nigh, being justified by faith, having peace with God—made nigh, being adopted into the family of God and made the children, the sons and the daughters of the Lord God Almighty.

We also have need of a Mediator who is a king. Although we may be reconciled to God, we still have enemies. And so we need him as a king to rule in us and over us. We have enemies because of our reconciliation to God. These enemies include 'the world that lieth in the wicked one'. He that is a friend of the world is an enemy of God: because the world is at enmity with God, therefore the world is at enmity with the people of God. They also have an Ishmael at enmity with the Isaac within their own souls. That which was born of the flesh, which was Ishmael, mocked Isaac, who was born of the Spirit. So that within the faculties of God's people's souls there is 'that which is born of the flesh', the old sinful nature, and 'that which is born of the spirit', the new creation, the new birth. These are opposed to one another, and therefore we need a king to rule over our inward enemies as well as to subdue our outward enemies.

Now we also need a prophet. There is an important difference between the function of a prophet and a priest. The priest, as I endeavoured to explain last week, appeared before God on behalf of the people. You remember, on the great Day of Atonement the priest laid aside the garments for glory and beauty, and clothed himself in the ordinary white linen garments of an ordinary priest, and in that way he stood alone before God, representing Israel. By contrast, the prophet stood before Israel on behalf of God.

As a prophet, Moses stood before Israel on behalf of God. God had something to say to them. To start with, as we read in Exodus, God spoke to Moses from Mount Zion, and Moses told them what God required them to do. What did they say? 'Oh,' they said, 'all that the Lord our God commandeth us to do, that we will do' (see Exodus 24). What words were these? They were the words of spiritual ignorance. It was the same darkness and the same ignorance as in the heart of the young ruler when Christ put to him the law of God. 'All these,' he said, 'have I kept from my youth up!' What ignorance! What darkness! And so Israel thought they were capable of doing 'all that the Lord commandeth us'. But then, as we read in Exodus 20, they heard the voice of God himself speaking from Mount Sinai. He gave them the ten commandments and it was a fearful experience. So what did they say now? Now they said, 'Let not God speak to us, or we die.' They were afraid to hear God directly. Instead, they said, 'Speak thou with us.' They wanted Moses to represent God to them.

In that, God said they had well spoken. Well spoken. It's good for you if you have learned that you cannot obey God's law, if you have learned that the law is holy and spiritual and good and that you are carnal, sold under sin. 'Let not God speak to us, lest we die, but instead let us hear his prophet representing him to us!' It is well spoken.

So instead, the prophet spoke to the people on behalf of God. Now it is necessary to have a prophet because of the sinful state of the people, and their ignorance and darkness.

In order for us to understand and to grasp the need of a prophet, we must come to the knowledge of ourselves. When Israel did not know themselves they said, 'Oh yes, all that the Lord our God commandeth us to do we will do.' They thought they were able to do it. They thought they had the spiritual capacity to keep the law of God. But they found out different, and it's when they found out different that they spoke better words.

Now the knowledge of ourselves has two branches that I may speak of. The first is the knowledge of what we were before we sinned. You cannot know yourself, and you cannot know anything about man, if you do not know what was true of man when he came forth from the hand of God to start with. All study of man that ignores this branch of knowledge means that man cannot be properly understood. That is why any philosophy, psychology, or psychiatry that is not based on the principles of Christianity cannot ultimately be profitable or give a true knowledge of man. We must know whence we have fallen.

This is something that we *can* know, in virtue of what the prophet Moses wrote. 'God spoke by Moses' when Moses wrote the book of Genesis, telling us the true account of the creation of the world, and the true account of the creation of man. This is very important for you and for me to understand, especially in a day when there is such darkness and spiritual ignorance that people believe the hypothesis of evolution, which is as much as to say that man is a glorified brute. Now that's spiritual darkness! They might be very learned scientists, and capable in all sorts of ways, but I'm not speaking about natural light, I'm speaking about spiritual light and spiritual knowledge. For people to believe these kinds of futilities is a sign of spiritual darkness. The two elements in spiritual darkness are the lack of spiritual light, and the lack of spiritual eyesight. A man may have the light of the sun, but if he is blind he cannot see it. So there is more required than spiritual light: spiritual eyesight, or spiritual discernment, is also required. Even if we are familiar with the spiritual truths which God has revealed, in our sinful condition we do not possess spiritual discernment. We are instructed in the scriptures, 'Remember now thy Creator in the days of thy youth.' But how can we obey this if we refuse to believe what the prophet Moses has revealed to us from God? How can young people obey this portion of the Word of God if they believe what they are taught in school and university, the falsehood of evolution?

Now, when Moses spoke from God, God was speaking through his Word—that is, his personal Word, Christ. Through the prophet Moses, Christ was exercising his own prophetic office, although he had not yet actually taken it up in the state of humiliation—he was revealing to us by his Word and Spirit the will of God for our salvation.

In Genesis we are given spiritual light on man's condition before he fell, and spiritual light as to how he fell, and the second branch of knowledge Genesis gives us is spiritual light on man's condition as he is after the fall—that he is a hell-deserving, ruined creature, a child of wrath even as others. This sinful, ignorant condition is what constitutes our need of a prophet. But who is able to meet this need? There are many false prophets: we don't need them. We don't need Mohammed—he knows nothing about it, and neither do his followers. No—the prophet that we have is 'a prophet, made like unto Moses'. The prophet we have is the Prophet promised by God, the one who is able to speak from God, the everlasting Father.

And this Prophet is able both to give spiritual light, and to give spiritual sight. There's no spiritual light apart from the Word of God. Men may claim to have what they call spiritual light, but it doesn't come from the Word of

God. Christ the Prophet says to them, 'If the light that is in thee be darkness, how great is that darkness!' But Christ gives spiritual light by opening up the Word of God. 'Did not our heart burn within us, while he talked with us by the way, and while he opened to us the scriptures?' Then we felt the light rising and dispelling the darkness of our souls. He gives spiritual light—and, more, he opened their understandings so that they might understand the Scriptures. The Lord gives the blind their sight—'in that purest light of thine / we clearly light shall see' (Psalm 36:9).

2. Christ is this Prophet

That brings me now to the Prophet who was promised and the Prophet who came, the Prophet who is alive, and alive for evermore. As the Lord Jesus Christ is like the apple tree among the trees of the wood, so he was the greatest of all the prophets. Not only was he fairer than the sons of men as King, but he was more glorious than the sons of men as Prophet also.

'Like unto Moses'. The apostle Paul in writing to the Hebrews compares Christ to Moses. He says that Moses was faithful over God's house as a servant. Now that is a tremendous testimony to that eminent man of God. Moses was one of the greatest men that the world ever saw, and was made so by the grace of God. But Moses was faithful as a servant in God's house, and Christ was faithful as a Son over his own house. So here is a distinction between Moses and Christ—it's between Moses the servant and Christ the Son. The Prophet who is promised here is the eternal Son of God. He dwells in the bosom of the Father—he dwells in the bosom of the Father's love, and dwells in the communion of eternal love between the Father and the Son and the Holy Ghost.

So he is one who knows the Father—he knows the Father as none other does. And he knows the mind of the Father as none other does. He was there in the counsels of eternity. Before the world was, he was there, as the eternal Son of God. In the counsels of eternity he was set apart to be the Mediator in connection with the purposes of the love of God, to save a number that no man can number—to save them from going down to the pit of destruction, and to bring them to everlasting glory.

Moses was eminent among the prophets. God appeared to other prophets in dreams and visions and so on, but with Moses, a special phrase is used: the Lord appeared to him 'face to face'. This expression, 'face to face', or 'mouth to mouth', means that Moses had a special nearness to God. Now we see that special nearness to God reflected when Moses came down from the mount—his face was shining with the spiritual nearness he had in his soul to Jehovah on Mount Sinai. The glory of it shone through his body, shone on his countenance. In Moses' case it was only momentary. That glory passed away. But here is one, and the glory of God shines in his face—it shines in his person, I should say—to all eternity. He is the brightness of the Father's glory. His communion with the Father is not a short time—a number of days on Mount Sinai—but it is an eternal communion on the mountains of eternity.

But here is the most important distinction between Christ and Moses. Moses spoke what God revealed to him. But when Christ speaks, he speaks from God in the sense that he *is* God: he is the personal Word of God.

But in this promise there is a great wonder. The Son of God, when raised up to be a Prophet, was to be raised up *from among the brethren*, from among the Church of God. As King he was raised up from among the people. 'Out of the folk I raised a chosen one' (Psalm 89:19). As Priest he was also raised up from among the people (Hebrews 5:1). And here also as Prophet he was raised up from among the brethren. In his incarnation, the Holy Spirit conceived a holy humanity so that, like his brethren, he would be partaker of flesh and blood. So when he would appear before the people, he would appear as the Son of God in your nature and mine, speaking the words of God in the words of men. What a glorious conception we have here of the Prophetship of the divine Redeemer.

Now, when you're reading about Christ, it's helpful to be asking yourself questions. And you *should* be asking yourself questions when you're reading your Bible and when you're hearing the gospel. So say this to yourself when you read about Christ, 'Now, here is the Saviour, and what office is he exercising here?' Well, let me give an example. Think of him in the 17th chapter of John, and after last Sabbath morning you can all say that as he was interceding he was exercising his priestly office. But what is he saying as he intercedes? When he is there exercising the priestly office he also refers to his prophetic office. He says to the Father, 'I have given unto them the words which thou gavest me ... I have given them thy word.' Compare this now to the promise in our text: 'I will raise them up a prophet from among their brethren ... I will put my words in his mouth; and he shall speak unto them all that I shall command him.' So in John 17, in fulfilment of the promise, the Prophet in our nature is saying to his Father, 'I have given them the words which thou hast given me.' The Father gave him words to speak to the Church, to the people, and these words he had given them.

Now he did this in his state of humiliation. While it is correct to say that he became a prophet when he was raised up from among the brethren, yet when we come to the question of when he started the public exercise of his prophetic office, we must go to the baptism of Jordan, where he began his public ministry in the world. When he was baptised by John at Jordan, John tells us that the Holy Spirit descended on him as a dove. He descended and remained—yes, remained, remaining forever upon this Prophet. And when that happened, the heavens were opened, and the voice from the heavenly glory said, 'Thou art my beloved Son, in whom I am well pleased: hear ye him.' The Father was well pleased with his beloved Son as the Prophet of his people. He gave the same testimony later on in the time of his humiliation, at the Mount of Transfiguration, when his glory was shining more gloriously than the glory that shone in the face of Moses when he came down from Mount Sinai. There's Moses, and there's Elias, that great prophet, the great prophet of revelation. (And how much we need the spirit of Elias now in 1991!) There the disciples saw the glory of this the greatest Prophet. The voice came from the heavenly glory, saying, 'This is my beloved Son, in whom I am well pleased.' And what else? What else? Here it is! Listen to it! 'Hear ye him!' Moses is gone. Elias is gone. But Christ is the same yesterday, today and forever: hear him! He is the Prophet: hear him!

We are to hear him speaking in his Word. We have now, in the Word of God, the words of Christ which he received from the Father. Do you

127

ever think of that? Did you ever think of this, when the Saviour speaks to your soul by the ministry of the gospel, and says in the written Word of God, 'Come unto me, all ye that labour and are heavy laden, and I will give you rest'? The Father gave him these words to speak—the Father against whom you have sinned, prodigal sons and prodigal daughters. The Father has told his Son, Say this to them, 'Come unto me, all ye that labour and are heavy laden, and I will give you rest.' These are the words of Christ, which the Father gave to him. 'I have given unto them the words which thou gavest me.'

Now this opens up a great field which I do not have time to enter into just now. I will just mention that when Christ exercised his office in the state of humiliation, he did so (as we say, speaking in theological terms) *immediately*. That is to say, he spoke himself without an intermediary, without any other mediator.

Think for example of how the woman of Samaria heard the voice of Christ. This was her own testimony of what happened: 'Come, see a man, which *told me all things* that ever I did: is not this the Christ?' Now, I think there is something very impressive about what the woman of Samaria says— although of course she is a most impressive convert for many reasons. As you know, the Samaritans were separate from the Jews, and they believed that the five books of Moses were the only scripture (not the psalms, or the historical books, or any of the rest of the Old Testament). So this poor woman of Samaria only had the Pentateuch to go on for knowledge about the Messiah. But this is what she said, 'I know that Messias cometh, which is called Christ: when he is come, he will tell us all things.' Is that not remarkable? He will tell us all things. This is just the portion that we are considering just now: 'He shall speak unto them all that I shall command him.' And so it was, that he gave his people all that the Father told him.

Of course this involves the whole of the Word of God, from Genesis to Revelation. It was all given by Christ through the inspiration of the Holy Spirit, with whom he was anointed without measure. There was Moses—he had the Holy Spirit in measure. There was Elias—he had the Holy Spirit in measure. There are Jeremiah, Isaiah, and all the prophets down to Malachi—they all had the Holy Spirit in measure. But this Prophet had the Holy Spirit without *measure*. So that when he speaks, you may be sure that you have the mind of God. You needn't go to Mohammed, you needn't go to the Pope, you needn't go to Buddha. This poor generation like a silly set of doves are flying all over the place (Hosea 7:11). But you needn't go anywhere else. You have in our Prophet, the Lord Jesus Christ, one who knows the mind of the Father in all its infinite, eternal, unchangeable extent. Moses only knew some of it. Jeremiah only knew some of it. And even Paul, though he was exalted to the third heavens, knew only a part of it. But Christ knows it all, and what they knew they received from him.

So Christ exercised his prophetic office in the state of humiliation immediately (without an intermediary). They heard the voice of Christ speaking to them with authority, with power. Now for some, the words of Christ were too hard. 'This is a hard saying,' they complained, 'who can hear it?' So they went away from him, and he never went after them. Solemn! Take you good care that that's not the last time you hear his voice until you hear it on the day of judgment, saying, 'Depart from me, ye cursed.' But he asked his disciples, 'Will ye also go away?' And Peter replied, speaking on behalf of them all, 'To whom shall we go? thou hast the words of eternal life.' That's where they got eternal life—in the words of Christ, in the teachings of Christ, in the doctrine of Christ. By the Spirit of Christ they got eternal life in their souls. But it was through the Word of God coming from this person who was exercising the office of Prophet in his state of humiliation.

3. Christ's work as the Prophet

Now when Christ was in his state of humiliation, there were many things he taught them which they did not properly understand. They did not properly understand about his death or about his resurrection—a full understanding of it didn't come till later. Nevertheless it remains true that when he was in this world in his state of humiliation, there were some who heard the voice of Christ and were brought to spiritual life. He said himself, 'The hour is coming, and now is, when the dead shall hear the voice of the Son of God: and they that hear shall live.' This is a voice which carries the words of eternal life into the soul. And even when he died—oh, his enemies thought his voice wouldn't be heard again, that the voice of Jesus of Nazareth would be silent in the grave. But the prophetic office of Christ did not come to an end any more than his priestly and kingly offices came to an end. And then he rose from the dead by the power of an endless life, and he told his disciples how he was to exercise his prophetic office in a state of glory. 'I will pray the Father, and he shall give you another Comforter' (John 14:16). And that Comforter is the Spirit of truth, and he would lead them into all truth (John 16:13). So in glory, Christ is still the Prophet of his people, exercising his prophetic office in sending the Holy Spirit as the Spirit of truth to instruct souls.

Now, I'm mainly concerned just now with one particular part of the prophetic office—how its effect is felt in this world (just as last week I was concerned with how the priestly office as exercised in heaven by way of intercession has its effects in this world). But I'd like to mention something else, and that is that I believe that Christ is in a sense also exercising his prophetic office towards the spirits of just men made perfect. The Lamb that is in the midst of the throne shall feed them, and lead them to fountains of living waters. That is to say that he is leading them into the greater depths of the wells of life that are in God—they will be drinking out of these wells, world without end—and that in the light not of grace, but of glory. Just as the Holy Spirit leads them into the truth in time, so there Christ will be leading them into the greater, fuller manifestations of divine glory in eternity. So the Prophet who was mighty in word and truth in time, is still mighty in word and truth even in heaven itself, as they grow in the knowledge of the glory of the Father, of the Son and of the Holy Ghost.

But for now, the main point is how he's exercising his prophetic office through the Holy Spirit in this world. This he does inside the Church of God. Now, there's a great deal of denigration of the Church at the present time. People are turning instead to para-church movements, thinking that these are the places where everything's happening. But this is a delusion. The Holy Spirit operates within the Church itself. Christ has promised to be with the Church itself till the end of time. 'I will never leave thee, nor forsake thee.' The main way he exercises his prophetic office in the Church today is by raising up preachers of the everlasting gospel.

Now, although the Church in Old Testament times had prophets, there is no longer the office of prophet in the New Testament Church. The prophecy, the forth-telling, which is part of the prophetic office, is now finished. In the New Testament, we no longer have the Church in the wilderness, but the Church in a settled state. In the New Testament Church Christ has instituted the ministry of the gospel, his ambassadors. The prophets stood before the people to speak the Word of God, but the ambassadors for Christ stand before the people to preach the Word of God from the mouth of Christ.

All who are ambassadors are *called* to that office. I was very much struck by the words about the Levites in our chapter—'If a Levite come from any of thy gates out of all Israel ... and come with all the desire of his mind into the place which the Lord shall choose; then he shall minister in the name of the Lord his God.' Now I believe that what took place in the case of the Levites also takes place in connection with ministers of the gospel. They are first of all called to be ministers of the gospel, but by the call of Christ, through the Holy Spirit, as the great Prophet of the Church, they are sent to the place where they are to preach as his ambassadors. He comes from any of the gates, wherever the gates are in the land, and he comes with all the desire of his mind to the place which the Lord chooses, and then and then only, he shall minister in the name of the Lord his God.

As the glorified Prophet, Christ receives gifts for men, and he gives these gifts to the Church by the Holy Ghost, in calling ministers to preach the everlasting gospel as ambassadors for Christ. Ministers are to stand before the people and give them the Word of God as it comes from Christ. This Word is the word of reconciliation. 'We pray you in Christ's stead,' say the ambassadors, 'be ye reconciled to God.' Look at the great Prophet himself, weeping over Jerusalem, and what is he saying? 'Oh Jerusalem, Jerusalem, how often would I have gathered thee, as a hen gathers her chickens under her wings, but ye would not!' 'Come unto me, all ye that labour and are heavy laden!' In Christ's stead ambassadors must beseech the people, gathering them to Christ, and through Christ to be reconciled to the everlasting Father.

Now, of course those who are called to the office of ambassador cannot do anything of themselves. They know that, and if they don't know that, they shouldn't be taking the office on themselves. Paul may plant and Apollos water, but it is God who gives the increase. The preaching must be accompanied by the power of the Holy Ghost. This includes the two things I referred to already—first of all there must be spiritual light, and secondly there must be spiritual eyesight to see in that light. God himself must command the light to shine out of darkness, and God himself must shine in our hearts. 'God, who commanded the light to shine out of darkness, hath shined in our hearts.' And how? By his Word. It's by his Word he still commands light to shine into people's hearts.

That's first of all the light of the law, to enlighten those who are still going about saying, like yourself and myself when we were in a state of nature, 'All that the Lord our God commandeth us to do, that we will do.' We were like the rich young ruler, 'We have kept all these commandments! We've been doing our best—we know we're all sinners and we can't be expected to do as much as perhaps we ought to do, but still, surely God is pleased with us—we're in church twice on Sabbath, we're at the prayer meeting, we have family worship in our homes, we hear the gospel, and so on.' And then there comes a ray from Mount Sinai—the voice of God—a ray of light from the law of God. And what's the law of God saying? 'The wages of sin is death,' and, 'the soul that sinneth, it shall die.' With that light shining, now the soul sees and says, 'I have sinned against heaven, and before thee.' That self-righteousness is banished out of the soul. No longer is that soul saying, 'All that the Lord our God commandeth us to do, that will we do'—rather, they see they're coming short with every breath they draw. Instead they're now saying this, and it's well spoken—can you say it yourself?—'The law is spiritual,'—holy, just and good—'but I am carnal, sold under sin.'

But then there is light of this second kind: spiritual eyesight. 'God who commanded the light to shine out of darkness, hath shined in our hearts, to give the light of the knowledge of the glory of God'—not in the face of Moses but 'in the face of Jesus Christ', in the person and work of the divine Redeemer. And the Saviour says with regard to the Holy Spirit, 'He shall glorify me: for he shall receive of mine, and shall show it unto you.' And so through the gospel the sinner can now come to see the beauty, the suitability, the fullness, the freeness of the salvation that is in Christ. The sinner is made willing to embrace him as all his salvation and all his desire, and so be saved in him with an everlasting salvation.

I've mentioned before, because I like it very much, the phrase used by an old man when he was speaking to the question on the Friday of a communion season on the Island of Lewis. 'The Lord's people will never forget how glorious the Holy Spirit made Christ to them in the gospel in this world.' They'll never forget it. They'll never forget it. Just like Ewen Cameron—as you remember, Rev Neil Cameron wrote a piece about him. When Ewen Cameron was dying, he asked to be carried out to see the hills and the valleys of his native Argyll. And when he had looked round he asked to be carried inside again, and this is what he said. 'It is', he said, 'a bonny world. But what made it a bonny world to me was that I found Christ here.' When he found Christ here it was in the gospel—it was in the Word of God. He found Christ, and that made it a bonny world. It is the same with some of you here this Sabbath morning. In spite of all your fears, and all your doubts, and all the hard things you write against yourself, you can say the same thing: 'His mouth'—Christ's mouth, the mouth of this Prophet—'His mouth is most sweet: yea, he is altogether lovely.' And therefore you can go on and say, 'This is my beloved and this is my friend' (Song 5:16). And don't be afraid of going on to say that! Don't let unbelief and the devil prevent you! If you can say, 'His mouth is most sweet,' then you can go on and say, 'This is my beloved and this is my friend, O daughters of Jerusalem.'

Now we come to the last matter, and it will not do to forget it. In the Acts of the Apostles we read how Peter spoke about the fulfilment of this prophecy. 'Moses truly said unto the fathers, A prophet shall the Lord your God raise up unto you of your brethren, like unto me; him shall ye hear in all things whatsoever he shall say unto you.' Remember the woman of Samaria—in all her darkness she got a hold of that. But here is what else Peter says, and I cannot say anything more solemn. 'It shall come to pass, that every soul, which will not hear that Prophet, shall be destroyed from among the people.' As surely as many hundreds of years passed after the promise in Deuteronomy and then this Prophet appeared in the world, so surely this will come to pass as well, that every soul which refuses to hear him—souls in St Jude's as well as others—shall be destroyed from among the people. There are those who hear his voice and they say, 'His mouth is most sweet.' But it shall come to pass that those who refuse to hear his voice shall be destroyed from among the people. It shall come to pass that, from the very lips from which others heard the words of salvation, the very lips from which others heard the Saviour saying, 'Thou art mine,' from these very lips will come the words to the unbelievers, the despisers of Christ, 'Depart from me, ye cursed, into everlasting fire'—everlasting destruction—and they will be destroyed from among the people.

Therefore let each one of us have a desire in our souls to hear the voice of Christ savingly. The voice of the great Prophet of the Church is saying to you and to me, 'Come unto me!' And, 'If any man thirst, let him come unto me, and drink.' 'Ho, every one that thirsteth, come ye to the waters!' The invitation is full, the invitation's free, from the lips of him who has 'the tongue of the learned … to speak a word in season to him that is weary.'

May he bless his Word. Let us call upon his name.

8 Seen of angels

1 TIMOTHY 3:16

And without controversy, great is the mystery of godliness: God was manifest in the flesh, justified in the Spirit, seen of angels, preached unto the Gentiles, believed on in the world, received up into glory.

Lord's Day morning, 15th April 1979

This statement by the apostle is in its own way a summation of the Christian faith. Many statements in the New Testament are of this nature, in which the apostle by the Spirit of inspiration brings before us (and before those who read the Word of God in every age and generation) a summary of the faith of the Church of God.

Lying at the basis of this faith is the fact that it is a mystery. Great is the mystery of godliness. The word 'mystery' here means (as it generally does in the New Testament) something which is revealed—something that could not have been known by man in the exercise of his natural heart, or the exercise of his natural intelligence. The exercise of man's natural powers of reflection could never have brought him to know the things which are revealed by God. Therefore the phrase 'the mystery of godliness' points to those particular things which could never have been made known unless God himself had revealed them. Man could not have attained to these things, he

135

could not have grasped them in the exercise of his natural intelligence and wisdom, but 'God hath revealed them unto us by his Spirit,' says Paul in another place, 'for the Spirit searcheth all things, yea, the deep things of God' (1 Corinthians 2:10). Therefore lying at the very basis and foundation of this summary of Christian doctrine is the fact that what we know of God, what we can come to know of God, must be revealed and made known by himself. This is because we are sinners, because we are ignorant, because we are brutish in our understanding, and because while we can grasp natural things and may show a great deal of ability in doing so, yet when it comes to the things of God, we are dark and ignorant. We do not understand these things, we have lost the knowledge of God, we can only come back to obtain that knowledge through the Word of God and especially through the revelation of God's mercy and grace in his beloved Son.

Now on this particular occasion we just wish to deal with one of the statements contained in this summary of the Christian faith. And that is the statement that the Saviour was 'seen of angels'.

1. Jesus was seen of angels

It seems at first sight a very remarkable thing to include this in the mystery of godliness. Not only that he was justified in the Spirit, not only that he was preached to the Gentiles, not only that he was believed on in the world and that he was received up into glory, but this is also told us, that he was seen of angels.

The angels saw Jesus at their creation

Now first of all we would remark that he was seen of angels at their own creation. Now of course there are many views as to when the angels were created, and it is not a matter on which one should be very dogmatic. What we do know is that they rejoiced at creation, that they were created certainly before the creation of man, that they were created by God as spirits, without bodies, and that they were created as a set of beings altogether glorious in themselves. And they were created to serve God, to praise God, and to rejoice in the glory of God.

In connection with all this, they saw the Son of God. Christ is the personal Word of God, and we are told with regard to him, as the personal Word of God, that 'all things were made by him; and without him was not anything made that was made' (John 1:3). We are also told with regard to the Son of God that he is the brightness of the Father's glory (Hebrews 1:3). That is to say, all the glory of God that shines outside the Godhead shines in the person of the Son. Therefore when the angels were created—in the moment they were created—the first person they saw was the Son of God. The first glory that they saw, and the first glory that illuminated their spirits, was the glory of God in the person of the Son of God. As the Father through the Son and by the Holy Spirit brought these beings into existence, as holy beings filled with divine light and love, so they saw the glory of God in the person of the Son of God. In their first sense of being conscious in being, they saw the glory of God in the person of the Son.

The angels saw Jesus at his incarnation

Now the next thing we would like to take notice of is that when these angels saw the glory of the uncreated God, and the glory of the eternal Son of God, they knew and had some understanding of the love wherewith the Father loved him, and the love with which they themselves loved him, and they glorified the Father in him. There came a time when they saw this person (as they told the shepherds) as one who was born in the city of David. This glorious person—in whom they had seen the first rays of the glory of God from the first time of their existence—they saw him now (as they had foretold) as one who was to be conceived in the womb of the virgin Mary, and they saw him as a child to be laid in a manger, and they were to see him there as God manifest in the flesh. They were to see their Lord as a babe. They were to see their Lord in the stable surrounded by the brute creation. They were to see their Lord lying as a babe, wrapped in swaddling clothes, lying in a manger, because there was no room for him in the inn. With regard to that sight they had a song, and that song was: 'Glory to God in the highest, and on earth peace, good will toward men.' That was the song which the angels sang, seeing the Lord of glory as a babe in the manger (Luke 2:14).

Why should they be singing of peace on earth? Why should the angels sing such a song when they had seen man fall in the Garden of Eden? Peace on earth had been destroyed. They had seen Adam and Eve driven out of the garden because of their sin. They had seen the whole human family born in sin and shapen in iniquity, in a state of rebellion against the God of heaven, adding sin to sin, treasuring up wrath against the day of wrath. Yet here they are saying, 'Glory to God in the highest, and on earth peace.'

That peace between God and man sprang out of the good will of God, the good pleasure of the God of heaven. It could come from nowhere else. All the ideas that men would like to return to God are all sheer fantasy. The god they would like to return to is a god of their own making, a god who would let them do what they like, a god who would let them satisfy the lust of the flesh and the lust of the eyes and the pride of life, and yet let them escape the death due to their sins. There could be no return to God, there could be no peace on earth, unless that arose in the good will of God, in his sovereign and gracious love to a number that no man could number. And that peace could not be obtained in any other way than by what the angels saw in Bethlehem. What the angels saw in Bethlehem was the Lord of glory in a holy humanity, the Lord of glory having joined to his divine person the humanity of a babe, and that humanity veiling his divine glory, as the Prince of Peace who was to work out peace between God and man, the Solomon of the New Testament.

And when the angels saw him, they sang that God was to be glorified in the highest. That expression, 'in the highest', does not merely mean that he is the high and the lofty one that inhabiteth eternity (Isaiah 57:15). It means glory to God in the sense that this is the highest revelation of God's glory. They had seen his glory when they themselves were created, when their intelligences were flooded with the view they had of the glory of God, when their spirits were warmed by the outgoings of love to themselves from the heart of God. They had also seen the glory of God in Mount Sinai, when the law was given. The glory that surrounded Mount Sinai caused the children of

Israel to say to Moses, 'Speak thou with us, ... let not God speak with us lest we die' (Exodus 20:19). But far greater than the glory of God in condemning sin, and far greater than the glory of God in the ministry of condemnation, is the glory of God in the face of this babe, in the person and in the work of Christ. In bringing peace on earth there is a glory which excels every other manifestation of God's glory.

Now, when the angels saw the glory of this babe, when they saw his glory as he lay in the manger, when they discerned that this was their Lord, when the angels saw the one in whom the glory of God shone, now veiled with this humanity—with this sinless humanity—conceived by the power of the Holy Ghost in the womb of the virgin—what a wonder it was to them! What a wonder! What a wonder it ought to be to us also! For if we could only see and know some of the glory of this person then we could understand why the angels desired to look into this.

The angels sang not only glory to God in the highest, and peace on earth, but also good will towards men. Good will, not towards the angels who kept their first estate, but towards men—sinful men, hell-deserving men, wicked men, men who are the children of wrath even as others.

What a view they got of their Lord at the incarnation!—these swaddling clothes, this holy humanity, as he lay an apparently helpless babe, and they knowing that at the very time he lay there, this divine person in glory was upholding all things by the word of his power. The Lord of glory would be born, not in a king's palace but in a manger, in a stable, the inn closed, the door closed—no place for the babe that was in the womb of Mary but to be born and laid in this manger!—born outside the place where the world were enjoying their fellowship, their companionship, their drinking, their songs, their enjoyment. To the angels these things would have been sheer vanity. Here was divine reality.

The angels saw Jesus in his sufferings
He was seen of angels with regard to his sufferings. Here was a very wonderful thing. These angels who saw him at his birth, these angels who

139

saw him in his holy humanity, the angels who undoubtedly saw him as he grew in wisdom and stature, in favour with God and with man: they also saw him in his sufferings.

We read in connection with the Garden of Gethsemane that an angel comforted him. Dr Duncan said, in his own usual unique way, that of all the angels, the one he most wanted to see in glory was the angel that comforted Christ in the garden. That angel saw Christ in his sufferings, in the Garden of Gethsemane. He saw him there stretched on the earth that he himself created. He saw him there with his sweat as great drops of blood falling to the ground, as in agony of soul he cried unto him who was able to save him from death. What a view that was to that angel! God the Father said, 'Let all the angels of God worship him' (Hebrews 1:6)—worship this person here, this person in the Garden of Gethsemane, this person who is saying to his Father, 'Father, if it be possible, let this cup pass from me' (Matthew 26:39). The cup of death. The cup of sorrow. The cup that caused him to say, 'My soul is exceeding sorrowful, even unto death.' That sinless soul, that sinless body, now fearing and trembling in the presence of this awful death. This death which none could endure but himself alone. This death in which his body was to be pierced. This death in which his soul was to be bruised. All this was already taking place, as he began in a special way to drink this cup of sorrow and death.

The angels saw him. What wonder it must have occasioned them to hear this person say, 'the cup that my Father gave me'! They had enough insight into the wonders of the love of the Father to his Son to be amazed at this, that the Father who loved his Son as he loved him was giving him a cup—and not the cup of love, but the cup of sorrow and the cup of death, which the sins of his people had filled. The Father was saying to his Son, 'This is the cup of death which belongs to thy people, and drink this cup thou must.' That was the answer. 'Father, if thou be willing, remove this cup from me,' the Saviour had said, 'nevertheless, not my will, but thine, be done' (Luke 22:42).

He was seen of angels. Oh, my dear friend, how they must have been filled with consternation, filled with wonder, at seeing the Lord of glory in his holy humanity being broken and under the sentence of eternal death and under the enduring of the eternal wrath of God against the sins of his people!

He was seen of angels. I very much agree with Hugh Martin's interpretation of how the angels strengthened the Saviour. That is, as he said, when God sent the angel to the Garden of Gethsemane, he sent him with this command in his heart, 'Let all the angels of God worship him.' And the Lord Jesus Christ—in the midst of all his sufferings, in the midst of his soul being exceeding sorrowful, even unto death—he found this angel worshipping him. What a wonderful thing that was! The Jews turned against him. The Roman soldiers and the Roman power were ready to arrest him and bring him to the cross of Calvary. The whole human race were joining hand in hand to despise the one who was born as a babe outside the inn. He was now to go outside the city of the great king, he was now to be crucified on Calvary's tree, and when this all took place, as he said to his disciples, it was the hour of the power of darkness. Shortly these powers were to come into the Garden of Gethsemane, and when the question was to be put to them, 'Whom seek ye?' they were to say, 'Jesus of Nazareth.'

In the midst of it all, here was this glorious being, this angel, and he worshipped him. He acknowledged the God of heaven, Jesus of Nazareth. He acknowledged the Son of God. In that worship the angel was as much as saying, 'Although there are thy sufferings, I have seen thy glory. I saw it when I was brought into being in this world, and I see it still in some measure now, though I cannot enter into how it is that the eternal Son of the Father in truth and love is suffering the way that he is suffering.' Nevertheless he worshipped him and so the Saviour was strengthened in the midst of his sorrows, in the midst of the sorrows of Gethsemane's garden, in the midst of the trembling of his human nature at the prospect of eternal death. This angel saw him and he saw this angel, and the angel strengthened him by obeying the divine command, even in the darkness of Gethsemane's garden.

But all the angels of God worshipped him, and they saw him, not only in Gethsemane's garden, but also as the one who suffered and died, who paid the great ransom price that none could pay but himself alone. He paid that price in love to lost and ruined sinners—with love to the very disciples who forsook him and fled—with love to those around the cross who at that time were crying, 'Away with him, away with him, crucify him.' The Saviour cast the garment of his intercession over them and said, 'Father, forgive them; for they know not what they do.'

And the angels saw redemption accomplished. When Lazarus died and his soul went out of his body into heaven, the angels of God were his companions going there. However much the angels had to do with this when the Saviour died, we cannot say. But we do say that the angels saw that when the Saviour said, 'It is finished,' redemption was accomplished. They saw that salvation was secured for sinners lost, ruined and undone. He breathed out his soul into the hands of his Father. 'Father,' he said, 'into thine hands I commend my spirit' (Luke 23:46). He breathed out his soul into the hands of the everlasting Father and into the bosom of the Father's everlasting love, and he left his body to be put in the tomb of Joseph of Arimathea. I read a very beautiful expression and a very beautiful thought in one of the old divines with regard to the tomb of Joseph of Arimathea. This old divine used the expression 'a virgin tomb'. No man had been laid there, no man had ever been laid in that tomb—it was, as it were, a virgin tomb. He said that this person who was born from a virgin womb came to have his body laid in a virgin tomb. And that was seen of angels. That holy humanity was conceived in a virgin womb, and after the death on Calvary's tree, after the accomplishment of eternal salvation, his body was borne by his people and laid in a tomb in which man had never before been laid. It was a virgin tomb for the body that came out of a virgin womb. What a very wonderful thing!—a wonderful thought and a wonderful expression!

The angels saw Jesus at his resurrection
That brings me now to this, that he was seen of angels at his resurrection. The angel that rolled away the stone was an angel that sat upon the stone, and the angels saw Jesus at his resurrection, when he rose from the dead by the power of an endless life.

He was seen of angels. They said to the women, 'Fear not ye: for I know that ye seek Jesus, which was crucified. He is not here: for he is risen, as he said. Come, see the place where the Lord lay' (Matthew 28:6, 7). 'Come and see what we are seeing, we who have seen the resurrected Jesus—see an empty tomb, see the triumph of the one who died, see the triumph of the one who suffered, see the triumph of the one who was wounded for the transgression of his people—see now that the grave is empty!'

You remember that when the grave was empty, the grave clothes and the face cloth (the napkin) were folded and laid in their place. That was to show that the person who rose from the dead was the captain of our salvation and that he was the captain of death. He was the one who had said in the ancient prophecy, ringing down the corridors of the centuries, 'I will ransom them from the power of the grave; I will redeem them from death: O death, I will be thy plagues; O grave, I will be thy destruction: repentance shall be hid from mine eyes' (Hosea 13:14). He folded up the graveclothes to manifest and make known in the first place that he disrobed himself of the clothes of death. He folded them as one who was completely triumphant. It was also to signify to his people that they would need to be clothed with death until the morning of the resurrection, when time shall be no longer.

The angels saw Jesus at his ascension

He was seen of angels at his ascension. We were singing of that in Psalm 68. 'Thou hast ascended on high.' When Christ entered glory, the people of God—Abraham, Isaac and Jacob and all the spirits of just men made perfect around the throne of God—would have sung as we were singing in Psalm 24, 'Ye gates, lift up your heads; ye doors, / doors that do last for aye, / Be lifted up,' so that the King of glory may enter into his place. And do you not think, my dear friend, that as the angels went up with the ascended Christ, the one who passed through these heavens into the sanctuary above—do you not think that the angels joined in that song as well? Well, I am sure that they did. They joined in that song as well. They called upon the doors, the doors that do last for aye, to lift up, and they called on the gates to lift up their heads, so that the King of glory might come to his place. The King of glory coming to his place was Jesus, the Son of God in our nature, and that nature now glorified.

The angels will see Jesus at the Day of Judgment
He will be seen of angels also at the Day of Judgment. The angels will form the train of Zion's King. They will surround the glory and reflect the glory of the Father in the person of the Son when he comes 'to judge the world in righteousness, judgment to give each one'. And these eyes that see me now, and these ears that hear my voice, it's Jesus that you will see. And it is Jesus who the angels will see when he comes to ascend the great white throne, to judge the world.

When he comes, he will use the angels in connection with that work, to separate the sheep from the goats, and to gather in his elect from all places of the earth on the resurrection morning. The angels will have their own place with regard to the glory of the great white throne and the solemnities of the final judgment, when for all eternity the complete and final separation will be made between those whose hope and confidence was placed in Christ alone, and those who loved the world and its ways and its pleasures and its vanities.

Christ will say to the one, 'Come, ye blessed of my Father, inherit the kingdom prepared for you from the foundation of the world.' To the others he will say, 'Depart from me, ye cursed, into everlasting fire, prepared for the devil and his angels.' Then Christ and his Bride shall be gathered at God's right hand, and they'll sit down to the marriage supper of the Lamb. And can we not also say that when the angels see the marriage supper of the Lamb, although the angels themselves cannot sit down at that supper, surely they will see it and they will rejoice in it? Part of their heaven will be rejoicing with the Bridegroom, as John the Baptist said. 'He that hath the bride is the bridegroom: but the friend of the bridegroom ... rejoiceth greatly' because he hears the bridegroom's voice. That applied to John in a particular sense, but will not the angels and the archangels and the cherubim and the seraphim also rejoice with joy unspeakable and full of glory when they see Jesus, the

Bridegroom of the church, and his Bride complete? 'They shall be brought with gladness great, / and mirth on every side, / Into the palace of the King / and there they shall abide' (Psalm 45:15).

2. Have we seen Jesus?

Now that brings me to this point in the second place: has he been seen by us? Have we seen Jesus?

Our seeing of him is in nearly every aspect of the case different from the way in which he was seen by angels. The angels referred to here are without sin—they are those who desire to look into the mystery of godliness, who desire to look into the revelation of God's mercy and grace in his beloved Son. But they have no need of mercy, they have no need of the forgiveness of sins, they have no need of being illuminated by the Word of God and by the Spirit of God. These spirits are the elect angels, they are the angels who have retained their first estate, and who have been confirmed in that estate and who enjoy the knowledge of that confirmation.

As you know, there were angels who 'kept not their first estate'. They fell, by sinning against God. They fell in union with one another, and they are reserved in chains of darkness against the judgment of the great day. From being angels of light they became spirits of darkness. But the angels who did not fall, they knew perfectly well and understood perfectly clearly that the angels who fell were created in the same way as themselves. They too were created holy spirits, in the possession of the knowledge of God, and indeed one of them, the prince of them, whose name was Lucifer (which means a bearer of light—in his particular service to God in his original creation, he bore about the light of God's glory)—Lucifer became, as he is now, the prince of darkness. Therefore the angels who retained their first estate needed to have it revealed to them that they were elect angels, and that they would never fall. That was done in connection with the headship of the Saviour, so that when they look upon Jesus alone, they see him as the head of the angels as well as the head of the Church. And they know that through him they are elect—through him they will never fall—through him they will

145

retain their happiness, their holiness, their enjoyment of the fellowship of God, their enjoyment of discerning the glory of God. This is a large part of their heaven, as it is a large part of the heaven of the spirits of just men made perfect. However, the case is very different with us, for we are sinners.

Therefore the question is very serious for us: 'Have we seen Jesus?'

Have we seen the Jesus of whom Paul spoke when he said, 'We see Jesus, who was made a little lower than the angels for the suffering of death'? Well, in order that we may see Jesus spiritually, we must see him in connection with the mystery of godliness. In other words, we must see Christ in the Word of God.

Now you remember when the Saviour was teaching his disciples that he was to leave them, and especially after he rose from the dead, he told them that from then on, they would need to know him by faith through his Word. You read in the case of Mary Magdalene, when she saw Jesus she did not know him first of all, but when he spoke to her and said, 'Mary,' then she recognised him and said, 'Rabboni.' Apparently she made as if to take hold of the Saviour. But he said, 'Touch me not.' Why did he say that? On the other occasion the women laid hold of his feet and worshipped him and he did not say to them not to touch him. But he said it to Mary Magdalene because of the intensity of Mary's love and the intensity of Mary's desire to enjoy the fellowship of her Lord as she had had it before. Mark that—as she had it before—as she said, 'They have taken away my Lord, and I know not where they have laid him.' The Saviour said, 'Touch me not … but go to my brethren, and say unto them, I ascend unto my Father and your Father; and to my God, and your God.' The fellowship which Mary was now to enjoy with the Saviour was not a fellowship in which she would see Jesus with the eyes of the body, but one in which she would see Jesus with the eyes of faith.

Then we have the incident with the two on the way to Emmaus. They were cast down, they were sad, and their sadness was seen on their countenance. When the Saviour drew nigh to them they said, 'We trusted that it was he which should have redeemed Israel.' But now—now we cannot see him any more, now he is in the grave's devouring mouth, now our hope is low—very low indeed, and as dark and cold as the grave itself. Then you see what the Saviour did. 'Ought not Christ to have suffered these things, and to enter into his glory?' he asked. They needed a spiritual view of the sufferings of Christ, and therefore he began to open up to them the Old Testament Scriptures where Christ was made known—and the Old Testament Scriptures, of course, are full of Christ. And as he did this, this is what they had to say: 'Did not our heart burn within us, while he talked with us by the way, and *while he opened to us the Scriptures?*' He opened to us the Scriptures, and this is where we are to see him today.

Here then is a question, whether the Lord ever spoke to us. Now many of the true people of God, who are very tender in their souls, sometimes worry about this. They say, 'Well, I cannot say that I've got any particular portion of the Word of God which I felt that the Lord spoke to me.' Now the point is that if the Lord spoke to you in *any* part of the Word of God, whether or not that was in a particular portion, the way that he spoke was opening up that portion to your understanding. He opened up the truths in that portion to your soul. Whether it was one portion, or whether it was a sermon, or whether it was a chapter, or whether it was a sermon you read, or whatever it was, whatever Christ speaks to the soul by the Holy Spirit, the nature of the speaking is, 'Did not our heart burn within us, while he talked with us by the way?' That's what he did. And then they saw Jesus in the Scriptures. They saw Jesus in the Scriptures that manifested him in this way, that Christ ought to have suffered these things and to have entered into his glory.

Therefore, when the question comes to us, 'He was seen of angels, has he been seen of us?' then the place where we must see him is in the Scriptures. The place where we must see him is in the Word of God. The place where we must see him is in the gospel of the grace of God.

Now that involves this, that we see ourselves. You will remember the very simple and very instructive tale of Hector MacPhail. When he was travelling down from Nairn to the Assembly, he stopped in a certain place and he was going to hold family worship. When the household gathered, he asked if everybody was there. There was this girl, a kitchen maid, who was not there, so he made sure that she was brought in. When he was setting off on his journey again, he bade her goodbye, and he gave her this prayer, 'Lord, show me myself.' When he came back some time later, he found her that she had indeed seen herself and it had caused her pain and sorrow. He then gave her the prayer, 'Lord, show me *thyself*.'

Now between these two prayers, you have the experience of the sinner in coming to see Jesus. First of all the sinner comes to see himself or herself in the light of God's Word as a sinner, without God, without hope in the world, without any possibility of delivering oneself from one's sins. And then the sinner comes to see Jesus as the Son of man who came to seek and to save that which was lost. The gospel becomes good news, in the sense of the term that it is bringing peace to sinners, the peace of God wrought out by God's beloved Son.

Have we seen ourselves? Have we seen that we are guilty, that we are lost, that we are ruined, that we are undone, that we cannot deliver ourselves? Has it caused us sorrow? Has it caused us grief? Has it caused us concern so that our question is, What must we do to be saved? Or, Is there salvation for a sinner such as I am?

Have we come to see that there *is* salvation for sinners? And if so, have we come to see that the Saviour is Jesus?—the same one who the angels saw, in the ways that we have been endeavouring faintly to describe. But my dear friend, although the angels saw him, and wondered, and desired to look into these things, they never saw Christ in the same way as Paul did, or as Peter did, or as the woman of Samaria did. 'Come, see a man,' said the woman of Samaria, 'which told me all things that ever I did,' and a man who revealed himself to me as the Messiah—the man who said to me, 'I that speak unto thee am he.' Well, there was a woman in the city who was a sinner, and when she came to the feet of Jesus, there was nothing she could do but have a flood of tears. Do not believe that she meant it to be so. Evidently she felt deeply indebted to the Saviour—her sins had been forgiven, and she loved much. She sought Jesus out, but when she came near to his feet, the tears flowed. It could not be otherwise, because they were the tears of love, and the tears of gratitude, and the tears of thankfulness, that these feet that she now washed with her tears and dried with the hair of her head were the feet that were to be pierced with the nails in order that her sins, which were many, might be remembered no more for ever.

So we need to see Jesus, Jesus as the Saviour, the one name given under heaven among men whereby we can be saved. And do you not agree with the two on the way to Emmaus, when they said, 'Did not our heart burn within us?' that there is a going out of your heart? There is a warming of your heart. There is a drawing in your affections to the Jesus whom you see in the Word of God, the Jesus whom you see in the preaching of the gospel of the glory of the blessed God. However dark you may feel on many occasions, yet when you hear about Jesus, do you not feel some warmth in your soul? When you hear about the one who said, 'Him that cometh to me I will in no wise cast out,' the one who said, 'I, if I be lifted up from the earth, will draw all men unto me,' then do you not feel a warmth that's not of this world? A fire kindled in your soul that doesn't come from this world at all.

I've often told this incident and it might be helpful to repeat it. One time I was staying with my aunt, the mother of the late Reverend Donald Malcolm MacLeod. I was staying down in a farmhouse near Killin, and I always remember, one morning, just like this morning, I came out of the house and I noticed above the door a nest, and this nest was just as black as one could possibly think of. And while I was watching it, the mother bird came along, flying along with a worm in her beak. And she began to give a call, and when she gave this call, the nest that had appeared so black became full of the open beaks of the fledglings who heard the call of their mother and who were now to be fed. I could not but compare that to how often I feel my heart to be, black and dead and earthly. But when the gospel is here, and when the joyful sound is heard, it awakens desires and longings, and the open beaks of these desires and longings looking towards Jesus.

Well, my dear friend, if that is true of you, you've seen Jesus. And you may as well stop worrying about it and doubting, because you can be as sure as you're sitting in your seat that if that is the case with you, that you feel these desires and these desires going out to Christ, then you *must* have seen him. 'Sir,' said the Greeks, 'we would see Jesus.' When the voice of Jesus is heard in the gospel of the grace of God, this dead soul of yours and mine feels the warmth and the reviving, and that is a clear and unmistakable sign that we have seen Jesus.

Also, if we have seen Jesus, it will leave in our souls a desire to see him again. 'They have taken away my Lord,' said Mary, but her desire remained: 'and I know not where they have laid him,' she said. But the Word of God says, 'O all ye that do seek the Lord, / your heart shall ever live' (Psalm 69:32). Those who have seen Jesus desire to see him again and again and again. They are on their way to heaven where they'll see Jesus, as the Lamb in the midst of the throne, world without end.

May he bless his Word. Let us call upon his name.

9 The still, small voice

1 KINGS 19:11-12
*And he said, Go forth, and stand upon the mount before
the Lord. And, behold, the Lord passed by, and a great and
strong wind rent the mountains, and brake in pieces the
rocks before the Lord; but the Lord was not in the wind:
and after the wind an earthquake; but the Lord was not
in the earthquake: and after the earthquake a fire; but the
Lord was not in the fire; and after the fire a still small voice.*

LORD'S DAY, 6TH OCTOBER 1979

We have an account given here of the prophet Elijah, who had been raised up at a particular time in the history of Israel. As you remember, after the death of Solomon, Jeroboam had been successful in taking away ten of the tribes from the rule of Rehoboam, who was left with the two tribes of Judah and Benjamin. The kingdom of Israel was thus rent in two. Jeroboam set up false worship among the ten tribes of Israel over which he was king, in order that they might not take the journey into Judah to go up to Jerusalem to worship at the temple. The consequence was that from the days of Jeroboam onwards, the ten tribes of Israel continued in a course of apostasy from the worship of God.

At the time of this king—Ahab, who was married to the notorious Jezebel—the apostasy had reached a very great height. Therefore this man

Elijah was raised up as a prophet to witness against the errors of Ahab and Jezebel and the priesthood of Baal. That work he had been engaged in just recently, when at Mount Carmel he had demonstrated to Israel in a very outstanding way that Jehovah was God and not Baal. Now, there is little doubt but that Elijah had expected that now there would be a great reformation in Israel and that they would return to Jehovah. But this did not take place. On the contrary, instead of these high expectations being fulfilled, he himself was threatened by Jezebel with the loss of his life. Therefore he had fled as directed by the angel and came to Horeb, the mount of God.

Horeb was the place where Moses had received the law. Elijah and Moses are often associated. On the Mount of Transfiguration Moses and Elijah met with the Saviour. These two men were outstanding in the Church of God and among the sons of God. They were both men of the same calibre, of absolute faithfulness to God, although as we can see and as we would expect, they had their times when their hearts fainted and when they came short. By this they proved that despite the wonderful grace they received and despite their previous faithfulness, they were still in this world—they were still men, still liable to fall and to be discouraged and to be cast down unduly.

1. The question put to Elijah
2. The revelation given to Elijah
3. The spiritual application of the revelation to ourselves

1. The question put to Elijah

We would like first of all to make a few remarks with regard to the question put here to Elijah, when the Lord asked him, 'What doest thou here, Elijah?' There he was in a cave in Mount Horeb, the mount of God. Whether or not this was the same place as the cleft of the rock into which the Lord put Moses (his great predecessor) when the Lord passed by, we are not in a position to say. Nevertheless, here he found a lodging place in the mount of God. And in this lodging place, where he felt the loneliness, the despondency, the disappointment after all that had taken place, he was asked this question, 'What doest thou here, Elijah?'

When Adam hid himself in the trees of the garden, the Lord said to him, 'Where art thou?' Similarly it was a voice that found Elijah. It found him in a cave in the mount of God and asked him, 'What doest thou here, Elijah?' Elijah tells the Lord what he was doing there. He said, 'I have been very jealous for the Lord God of hosts: for the children of Israel have forsaken thy covenant, thrown down thine altars, and slain thy prophets with the sword; and I, even I only, am left; and they seek my life, to take it away.'

Elijah was in the cave because he was jealous for the glory of God. He was in this cave in the hill of God because he was a man to whom the glory of God had been made precious. Here is a question for you and for me. Do we understand what it means for the glory of God to be made precious to us? Do we understand what it means for that glory to have been revealed and made known to us? Elijah realised and felt and understood something of the glory of God—as did Moses, his great forerunner, in whose face the glory of God shone when he came down from the mount of God (Exodus 34:29). These men, because they were men of God, were conscious of the glory that belonged to God. Their love for the glory of God is expressed in words such as these, that they were *very jealous* for his glory.

Now we cannot know anything about the glory of God unless it is revealed to us and made known to us. We cannot know anything about the glory of God unless the Holy Spirit of truth will shine his Word into our souls and into our consciences to give us to realise that God is glorious, that he has a glory that belongs to him. As Elijah felt, he has a glory which is above the glory of Baal and 'the idols dumb, which blinded nations fear' (Psalm 96:5). This was the God who was glorious, who was infinite, who was eternal, who was unchangeable, who was holy, just, wise, truthful, full of love and mercy and grace.

Elijah was jealous of that glory as it was revealed in connection with the worship of God. He says so here: 'The children of Israel have forsaken thy covenant, thrown down thine altars, and slain thy prophets with the sword.'

It was in the worship of God that this glory had been revealed before, in connection with the tabernacle—the place of meeting, where God met with his people, and where he said to Moses, 'There I will meet with thee, and I will commune with thee from above the mercy seat' (Exodus 25:22). That was where his glory shone. When the temple was constructed, the cloud of his glory came to dwell in the temple. Then, you remember, when they were carried away to Babylon, the prophet was given a view of the glory of God departing from the temple. This glory is bound up with the worship of God.

But as he says here, 'they have forsaken thy covenant, and thrown down thine altars.' The altars had been thrown down in the land of Israel, and false gods had been raised up. Jehovah had been forsaken and forgotten in the land. Baal was worshipped and King Ahab himself was now established in the worship of Baal as the official religion of Israel. All this was painful to this man of God, because he realised that it was in connection with the worship of God that God's glory was revealed. When we come to New Testament times, we no longer have the ceremonies of the tabernacle or the temple, but when we worship we come to the Word of God, we come to the throne of grace, we sing God's praises, we come to the sacraments of baptism and the Lord's supper. It is in connection with these means of grace that God's glory shines forth. Therefore the Psalmist prayed: 'That I thy power may behold / and brightness of thy face / As I have seen thee heretofore: / within thy holy place' (Psalm 62:2).

We see the footsteps of our God and our King in the sanctuary, for that is the place where his glory is made known. But in Elijah's time, the altars were broken down. The people had turned away from the worship of God and instead they were worshipping dumb idols. Elijah was feeling—and feeling it painfully—that the glory was departing out of Israel. He saw that glory to be an excellent thing. 'Sing unto the Lord; for he hath done excellent things: this is known in all the earth' (Isaiah 12:5). You see, my dear friend, if you ever come to know the glory of God, you will know it as something that is excellent. Nothing can be compared to it: to know God and to know the glory of God, to have his glory shining into our souls in the sanctuary, as

David prayed, 'Send forth thy light and thy truth; / let them be guides to me, / And bring me to thine holy hill, even where thy dwellings be. / Then will I to God's altars go, / to God my chiefest joy' (Psalm 43:3, 4)—God's altars are the place where that glory is revealed—the glory of holiness, justice, purity—the glory of mercy and grace and everlasting love.

Elijah also says, 'I alone am left.' It is plain from the narrative here that he was very cast down. He had just been on Mount Carmel, where he had challenged the people over how long they would halt between two opinions (1 Kings 18:21). If Baal be God, then let him be God, and if Jehovah be God, then let him be God. Let the thing be put to the trial. 'The God that answereth by fire, let him be God.' Remember how the prophets of Baal gathered— four hundred and fifty of them—but there was no fire from Baal to devour the sacrifice. They were left destitute of any evidence that Baal had any existence. But when Elijah built the altar to represent Israel, and when he put the sacrifice on the altar, then fire fell from heaven. The God that answereth by fire, let him be God! The people began to acknowledge this, that Jehovah, he is God. How promising it all seemed! Surely Baal's worship would now be overthrown? Were the ten tribes now to come back to Jehovah? Would they once more sing with the people of God: 'I joyed when to the house of God, / Go up, they said to me' (Psalm 122:1). Were they to go up with the people to Jerusalem once more to give thanks to the God of Israel?

No! The people had a momentary sense that God was Lord, that the Lord was God. Up there on Mount Carmel, overlooking the Mediterranean Sea, surrounded by all the beauty that is still on that mount, they were moved, but they were not changed. They were affected, but they were not regenerated by the Spirit of God. Therefore the reformation did not come. Instead of the reformation, Jezebel told Elijah that she would have his life.

Now we have no doubt that when Elijah fled, he was despondent, cast down, very affected by the situation. But we also think that there was more in it than that. We think he was concerned about this: if he were to be taken away, who would be left to witness on the side of God? 'They have slain thy prophets with the sword'—this was what Jezebel had done. Where would the witness in Israel be if Elijah was gone? He was saying, 'I am no better than my fathers,' and he asked to be taken away, but still, we believe, he was concerned about the cause and the glory of God in Israel.

Well, when he fled to the mount of God, he went into this cave. 'What doest thou here, Elijah?' Was this voice to be silent in Israel? Do you have to spend the rest of your days in silence? We have no doubt that Elijah was cast down by reason of manifold temptations. The people of God are cast down on many, many occasions. They are weak and feel weakened, they feel lonely, they feel sad, they feel cast down, they feel very often that their expectations are dashed—the expectations which burned so bright on the hills of their Carmels when they appeared to have a victory over the enemies of God, when the long looked-for reformation was to come. Instead of that, the enemy seemed to prevail again. Elijah felt this. They had broken the covenant, their souls were in danger. Israel as a nation was standing in the sight of God as ready to be given over to judgment. And so it eventually happened—they were scattered abroad so that they could not be found again.

Now when the people of God are so cast down, there is only one way in which they can be revived. Their prayer is, 'That in thee may thy people joy, / wilt thou not us revive?' (Psalm 85:6). You see, they cannot have joy apart from that. 'Restore unto me the joy of thy salvation' was the prayer of David (Psalm 51:12). They cannot have joy restored, they cannot have revival granted in the experience of their souls, apart from the Lord revealing himself and making himself known. 'What doest thou here Elijah?' Do we know anything about the Word of God finding us out? Do we know anything about the Word of God revealing where we are? Do we know anything about the Word of God revealing where we are with respect to God's glory and God's claim?

2. The revelation given to Elijah

Then when Elijah was on the mount of God, he was granted a revelation from God. As we read here, it came in the same way as Moses' revelation had—'the Lord passed by.' Elijah was commanded to go forth and stand upon the mount before the Lord, and he was given a very wonderful revelation. It was a revelation that contained a great many things which Elijah had to learn, in the condition which he was in and the work of a prophet which he was engaged in. Solemn things took place on this mount, as had taken place here before, in Moses' time, when the covenant was made on Mount Sinai. This hill of God had seen a solemn revelation of the divine majesty and divine glory. Here we have again solemn manifestations made, but we are told that God was *not* in them in a certain way, which we shall endeavour to notice. Let us therefore look at this revelation from the point of view of the history of Israel at this time.

This revelation is a most remarkable one, perhaps one of the most remarkable in the whole series of the Old Testament revelations. 'Go forth and stand upon the mount before the Lord,' he was told. It was in order that he might get a revelation with regard to the state of Israel, and also with regard to the end and purpose of his own work.

We think of Horeb, the mount of God. We think of Elijah the lonely figure standing on that mount. None of the tribes of Israel were there this time. When Moses was on the mount, the tribes of Israel were surrounding him in their thousands, ready to enter into covenant with Jehovah. But here was Elijah and here he was alone.

The first thing that he met with was 'a great and strong wind' which 'rent the mountains and brake in pieces the rocks before the Lord'. What a solemn moment this was! This lonely man standing before the Lord on the mount according to divine command, and seeing and hearing all this taking place. There was a sense in which the Lord was in that wind and there was a sense, as we read here, in which he was not. The sense in which he *was* in the wind was that this was a manifestation of divine power, a manifestation of the God of consummate holiness and purity. But there was a sense in which he was *not* in it, and that is, that he was not in it to bring Israel to repentance.

Again, after the wind, there was an earthquake. Now you know how earthquakes trouble people—they are called natural disasters—you know what a tremendous feeling of fear a person has when the foundation of the earth feels as it were departing. What a solemn and tremendous exercise of divine power it is! Yet God was not in the earthquake. He was in it, again, as a manifestation of divine power, but he was not in it with respect to bringing Israel to repentance.

Then after the earthquake, a fire—the flames leaping round the mount of God, the flames leaping around this man who stood on the mount, outlined against the sky. There was a sense in which the God who had answered by fire on Mount Carmel was here speaking by fire around the mount of God, but there was a sense in which he was not. Again, he was not in the fire to bring Israel to repentance.

Once he had received this revelation, Elijah wrapped his face in the mantle and went and stood in the entrance of the cave. The Lord said to him, 'Go, return on thy way to the wilderness of Damascus: and when thou comest, anoint Hazael to be king over Syria.' Hazael would be the great and strong wind, the rod of God coming down upon Israel for their sins and for their iniquities. God was in that with regard to his providence. God was in that anointing, so that this king of Syria would bring death and destruction upon Israel on account of their sins against God. But that judgment would not—and was not intended to—bring Israel to repentance.

Then Elijah was to anoint Jehu the son of Nimshi to be king over Israel. That was to be for the destruction of the house of Ahab, which had brought Israel to this its greatest pitch of idolatry and rebellion against God. Ahab's line was to be absolutely and completely swept away, and Ahab himself slain, and that judgment was to be made perfectly plain to the people of Israel. But God was not in that earthquake with regard to bringing the house of Ahab to repentance.

It was the same thing with regard to Elisha. He was to take over from Elijah in the office of prophet. Elisha was to prophesy destruction with regard to Israel. Anyone who escaped the sword of Hazael would be overtaken by Jehu, and anyone who escaped the sword of Jehu would hear the judgment that Elisha was to proclaim, that the Lord would slay them.

O what a sense of destruction! O the greatness of the evil of sin, the greatness of the evil of departing from God! What about us? What about

Scotland? Think about the First World War—the carnage, the loss of life, the destruction of the economy and all that was bound up with it. Did it bring us to repentance when Germany was used as the rod of God, after the prophets, the false prophets, the lying prophets of Scotland and England had drunk in the errors of Germany and spread them abroad and destroyed the worship of God in this land? God was in that judgment: but there was no repentance. Think of the Second World War—how we were brought just to the very brink of destruction, to the point where we were about to cease to be a nation altogether. That was by the power of Germany again, just as Syria was used as a rod against Israel.

The Lord used these two strokes to bring the children of Israel to realise the awfulness of sin, but they did not repent. So likewise with ourselves, we are still the same. We go further and further into idolatry, we go further and further into communion with the Man of Sin and with the false prophet and with idolatrous religion. God is not bringing us to repentance. After all the industrial strikes and all the winters of discontent, yet there is no sign of repentance. These are strokes from God—some of them like earthquakes and some spreading just like fire: but there is no sign of Britain coming to repentance, any more than Israel did, even though God is in these things, and even though the rod of God is evident in these things. God was not in them for Israel to bring them to realise their need of repentance. He smote them with starvation and with the sword and with plagues of every description and kind, and they still remained impenitent. God was in it all right—Elijah knew that God was in the wind, and God was in the earthquake, and God was in the fire, but he was not there to bring Israel to repentance.

You see that after this manifestation, Elijah says the same thing as before. When he heard the still small voice, he wrapped his mantle around him and went to the mouth of the cave. Then the Lord said to him the second time, 'What doest thou here, Elijah?' He said the same thing—'I am very jealous for the Lord God of hosts'—'but now I am seeing something that I did not see before'—that the Lord was not to be in these things to bring this people to repentance, that their hearts were to be hardened from the fear of God.

But the Lord was in the still small voice.

Now we are of the opinion that historically the still small voice relates to the seven thousand who did not bow the knee to Baal, nor kiss that idol. Elijah was concerned about this—'I only am left.' He did not know about the seven thousand. No wonder! He did not hear them. They were in the midst of the people. True it is, they did not bow the knee to Baal. True it is, they did not kiss the idol. True it is, they kept their hearts and sought to sanctify the Lord God in their hearts. But they did so quietly. Elijah was left alone. His was the only voice heard on Mount Carmel. Nevertheless I believe that these seven thousand prayed for him although he would not have known it. They would have seen that he would remain faithful, although he did not know they were there.

This was where the Lord was in Israel. Here was where the still small voice was, the voice of praise, the voice of the language of faith, the voice of those who still worshipped God in Israel and refused to have anything to do with the worship of Baal. Here was where the salvation of Israel lay. Isaiah would say likewise: 'Except the Lord of hosts had left unto us a very small remnant, we should have been as Sodom and we should have been like unto Gomorrah' (Isaiah 1:9). Elijah was told that they were there—they were still in Israel, they were on the side of Jehovah, even though they might not have been outspoken as this prophet was. Perhaps their voice had been the voice of gentleness. Perhaps they had not taken the public path that he was called upon to take. But still they were there, faithful to Jehovah. They would not bow the knee to Baal, nor kiss the dumb idols—their hearts, their thoughts, their affections were set upon Jehovah.

This is our only hope and expectation with regard to this land of ours, that there are still some who will not bow the knee to Baal—who will not kiss the false idols, who will have no part nor lot of any description or kind with breaking down the altars of Jehovah or interfering with the worship of God. That is where the Lord was—where the two or three were gathered together, and with the seven thousand who were living a life of faith upon the God of Israel and who also delighted in his ways, praying for the coming of his kingdom—and who undoubtedly upheld Elijah in the midst of all his tribulation.

Elijah was given to know all this as part of the revelation given to him. He was now drawing near the end of his days as a witness. He was soon to call Elisha, who would be anointed and appointed as the prophet who was to follow him. Elijah was a great man of God, an outstanding figure in the Old Testament history, the one who stood with Moses on the Mount of Transfiguration when Jesus of Nazareth was transfigured, when they spoke in heaven of the death he was to accomplish outside the gates of Jerusalem. He had penetrated even the hearts of the ungodly by his witness, and now he was getting ready to lay aside his prophet's garments. But there was a still small voice.

That should be an encouragement to us. It is not the loud bombast nor the pretensions of the modern profession of Christianity that is going to stand, but the still small voice of those who tremble at the Word of God—those who are on the side of Christ out and out—those who love the worship of God— those who love the day of God and the Christ of God. They were there in Israel and they were upholding the hands of Elijah, we believe. And Elijah, although he would not have known it, must have been a great encouragement to them. They were glad he was there. They were glad he was alive in that land of apostasy and they upheld his hands and strengthened him.

3. The spiritual application of the revelation to ourselves

In the third place let us look at this revelation from the spiritual point of view—what it means to the Church in every age and in every generation. We will look at what it means to the individual soul who comes to obey the voice of God which is calling the soul to come to the mount of God, and go and behold the Lord revealing himself and making himself known.

He was not in the wind, in a certain sense. And he was not in the earthquake, in a certain sense. And he was not in the fire, in a certain sense. Rather, he was in the still small voice. It was the same voice that was heard on the Sea of Galilee when the storm raged and when the waves came into the ship and when the disciples cried and said to the divine Redeemer, 'Master, carest thou not that we perish?' The still small voice said, 'Peace, be still,' and the waves were calmed, and they went in safety over Galilee in the peace that Christ gave. That is the great teaching which we have here: it is in the still small voice of the everlasting gospel that the sinner is to find peace with God. That is where you and I must find peace with God as well, in the one who said, 'Peace I leave with you, my peace I give unto you.' For the joyful sound is the still small voice.

You see, the judgments of God, unless they are sent in connection with the gospel, do not change men. Men only become hard under the judgments of God. They become sullen, they become rebellious under the judgments of God, unless the gospel is also there to point to them their sin and their iniquity.

Men will not read their own sins in the judgments of God. Where are the people who believe that the Second World War came upon Britain because of the sins of Britain? Instead they think we did very well. We fought alone! And so we did, but would we have fought alone if we had not been protected by prayer? When they were down there in Portsmouth facing the Germans on the other side of the Channel with only a few rifles between them, would we have succeeded without prayer? If Hitler had decided to cross the Channel instead of going off to Russia, we would have been destroyed, but instead a hook was put in his nose by the God of eternity, to lead him away in that direction.

People don't think of that—they don't say anything about it. They read about these things in history, and some of us know about it personally, but we do not stop to consider that this was all because of Britain's sins, Britain's iniquities. It's the same with all the trouble we are having now in connection with the Empire. People don't think of that. Britain was given colonies and brought the gospel to them along with many liberties. This is now forgotten and trouble has come as a result. O, their colonies have liberty? Some liberty they got from Amin! Some liberty they have from Kaunda and Nehru and the so called Frontline States like Angola and Mozambique! What is happening to the Christians there? They are being blotted out, that's what's happening. You don't hear that of course on the BBC, trying to keep up this façade as though there was something virtuous about Britain losing her empire. But the fact of the matter is that it is being lost because of Britain's sins, just as Old Testament Israel was weakened by enemy powers, and brought to face invasions again and again: they did not come to see it was because of their own sins. 'We with our fathers sinned have, / and of iniquity / Too long we have been the workers been; we have done wickedly' (Psalm 106:6). Neither could they see that without the gospel of the grace of God, without the still small voice of the one who said, 'Peace be still,' they would have been completely destroyed.

Now from the gospel point of view, when the Word of God is applied to the souls of sinners, there is very often something similar to what Elijah felt here on the mount of God. He was there alone, and the question was being put to him, 'What doest thou here, Elijah?' The Word of God was finding him out. He was surrounded by the evidences of the power of God. You see, when the Holy Spirit comes to work in a soul, the sinner is awakened by divine grace and brought face to face with the law of God by the knowledge of sins. The sinner is brought face to face with the power of God against whom he has sinned, the holiness of God against whom he has sinned, and the justice of God against whom he has sinned. When he is there, lonely in the mount of God, and with the Word of God speaking to him, the sinner is ready to conclude that there can be no hope for him. There is nothing that can appease God's claim. There is nothing that can ease the conscience awakened to a realisation of sin. There he is, alone with his sin, and he feels just like Israel did, when they were there, hundreds of years before, alone with their sins. And when they heard the voice of God, they said to Moses, 'Let not the Lord speak with us, lest we die' (Exodus 20:19).

Now, my dear friend, there is a sense in which God is in all that. God is holy, God is just, his law is spiritual, holy, just and good. There is a sense in which he is in this, that we should see our sins and our iniquities in the light of God's law. But there is no salvation in the law of God.

Whether we have this earthquake, whether we have these fires, whether we have the strong winds, whether we have the movements of divine power in a tremendous and solemn way or in a lesser, quieter way: there is no salvation in the law of God. The law holds forth no hope for any sinner. There is no salvation in the manifestations of divine judgment. There is nothing in these manifestations of judgment that will bring the soul to faith and repentance towards God. Faith in Christ and repentance towards God— it must come through the still, small voice of the everlasting gospel.

'Peace, be still.' The gospel is a voice speaking of stillness. It is a voice quietening the earthquake. It is a voice that quiets the winds and the fire. It is a peaceful, stilling voice. In that storm on the Sea of Galilee, when the waves came into the ship, the disciples asked, 'Master, carest thou not that we perish?' (Mark 4:38). The response was, 'Peace, be still.'

Have you been asking that question? Can you tell me of any time when you began to ask that question? Are you asking it now? 'Carest thou not that we perish?' The prodigal son came to see that he was perishing with hunger. And did not the trumpet sound in Assyria to those who were ready to perish? (Isaiah 27:13). Is it not for perishing sinners that Christ came? Christ is the one who can say, 'Peace, be still.' He is the one who can say this to the claims of God's law. He is the Son of God in our nature. He satisfied the claims of God's law, so that when the law of God comes into the soul with these claims, Christ can say, 'Peace, be still.' When the justice of God comes into the soul and says, 'Pay me what thou owest, for the wages of sin is death,' Christ can say, 'Peace, be still,' because when we were yet without strength, in due time Christ died for the ungodly. That's what the gospel is, the still small voice that speaks peace, that is, through the divine Redeemer.

The Saviour on Mount Calvary felt the earthquake and the winds and the storm of divine wrath encompassing him, so that he said, 'Save me, O God, because the floods / do so environ me, / That even unto my very soul / come in the waters be' (Psalm 69:1). He is the one who says to every sinner who looks by faith to him, 'Peace, be still.' Is this where you get peace? Is this where you got peace?—in the gospel revealing Christ, the Holy Spirit taking of the things of Christ and revealing them to the soul? What peace there is for the soul who is drinking in Christ in the everlasting gospel!—drawing water with joy out of the wells of salvation, drinking in Christ and enjoying doing so. When Christ says, 'Peace, be still,' there is a great calm. What a calm he sends to the claims of the law and the justice of God! Now the soul sees these claims to be fulfilled, and now these thunderous claims pass away, when the voice of the Saviour says, 'Peace I leave with you, my peace I give unto you. Let not your heart be troubled, neither let it be afraid.'

Elijah needed this revelation at this time in history. He needed to see and to understand that these judgments would not bring Israel to repentance. He now saw in a fresh way what Moses had seen before him, that 'The Lord our God is merciful, / and he is gracious, / Long-suffering, and slow to wrath, / in mercy plenteous' (Psalm 103:8). That is what brings the sinner down to sorrow over sin, to believe in Christ, and to trust in him forever. This is what took Elijah out of his cave and set him back on the path of duty.

Now, we are here contemplating the Lord's supper and commemorating in our congregation the death of the Saviour. It may be that you have some cave that you are hiding in. 'What doest thou here, Elijah?'

'Oh,' you say, 'I am living in a dark day, religion is very low.' If you have come to Christ and tasted that the Lord is gracious, will you not listen to the still, small voice? In connection with the Lord's supper, do you not hear this from the still, small voice?—'This do in remembrance of me.'

You may be here and you may be saying, 'If I had a wonderful sign, then I would commemorate Christ's death,' or, 'If I could but stand on the hill of God,' or, 'If I could but see some remarkable sign.' Well, Elijah saw all these signs, and the Lord was not in them. No! In fact Elijah was to learn that he had to do his duty—he had to go back to Damascus and anoint Hazael king of Syria, and so on—and that if he was to accomplish this, he was to be obedient to the Word of God through the still, small voice.

So many people seem to be of this mind—if only they would get some sign, some striking event, some striking experience, *then* they would commemorate Christ's death. They are waiting for *something*, but the Lord is not in it, my dear friend. The Lord is here in this still, small voice, 'This do in remembrance of me.' If you won't do it because of that, then you won't be doing it at all in a right way. You may think you are, and others may tell you that you are, but the fact remains that this is the word which we must obey, 'This do in remembrance of me.'

If we belong to the people of God, if we have been to the mount of God, if we have been to Mount Horeb, if we have come to know and to understand the still, small voice of Christ in the everlasting gospel drawing our souls into union and communion with himself, then this is what we must listen to—this still, small voice saying, 'This do in remembrance of me.'

May he bless his Word. Let us call upon his name.

10 The Prince's daughter

SONG OF SOLOMON 7:1

How beautiful are thy feet with shoes, O prince's daughter!

SATURDAY OF A COMMUNION SEASON, 11TH NOVEMBER 1995

The Song of Solomon is a book that sets before us the fellowship and communion which Christ, the great Bridegroom of the Church of God, has with his Bride, the living Church of God. That communion and fellowship is based upon the knowledge that they have of one another and the love that they share between one another. By the inspiration of the Spirit of God, this book brings before us the views that the Church has of Christ, and the views that Christ has of the Church. As enabled, this afternoon I would like to deal with the beauty that Christ sees in his Church when he says, 'how beautiful are thy feet with shoes, O Prince's daughter.'

We see that Christ addresses her as the Prince's daughter. She was in his view a person of great dignity. As his Bride, she was a person very precious to himself. That is true of all the spiritual members of the spiritual Church of God. For it is not the visible church of God that is being spoken of here but the invisible or the spiritual church—the true people of God who make up the members of the spiritual body of Christ.

But this was not the first view that he had of her, nor were they the first words that he addressed to her. We were reading Psalm 45 earlier, and the first words that he addressed to her there are, 'O daughter, hearken and regard, / and do thine ear incline; / Likewise forget thy father's house, / and people that are thine.' At that time she was in her father's house. All the souls who make up the Bride of Christ are members of the human family, and the Saviour described them elsewhere as being 'of your father the devil' (John 8:44). This is the place where they all were. This is where you and I are, as we are by nature. We are in the house of Satan, we are in the kingdom of darkness, that's where our companions are, that's where our lusts are fulfilled. That is where all the people of God were, along with the other members of the human family. They were in the house of their father the devil, and they were engaged in serving him. They were led captive by him at his will, and they were serving diverse lusts and pleasures, adding sin to sin and treasuring up wrath against the day of wrath.

Yet from among this vast multitude of souls in the house of Satan, and under Satan's power and reign, were those who were to make up the Bride of the Son of God. That is one of the great wonders that angels desire to look into. When God the Father chose a Bride for his beloved Son, he passed by the angels of glory, that myriad of angels who were created by his divine power and who kept their first estate. Although they were serving God with outgoings of perfect love and zeal, delighting in the service of God, they were all passed by. Instead the Bride of Christ was chosen from among the lost, the ruined, the guilty and the undone children of men, each of whom were by nature in the house of the kingdom of Satan and serving diverse lusts and pleasures. That's where they once were, but, to use the homely phrase of Thomas Boston, 'Although she was once a scullery maid in the house of Satan, now she is the King's daughter.' She is the Prince's daughter, the daughter of the Prince of Peace, and she is the King's daughter.

The Bridegroom of the Church took on the cause of those who were by nature lying in the dust and on the dunghill of sin. They were lost and ruined and hell-deserving and undone, with no spiritual beauty of any kind, having lost the image of God and now bearing the image of Satan. Yet they were the ones who were chosen and set apart by God the Father to be the Bride of his beloved Son. And the Son of God, the one whom the Father delighted in from all eternity, was himself willing that they should make up the Bride that he would have throughout the endless ages of eternity.

Before the Bride could be addressed as the Prince's daughter, she would need to be beautified. She was unable to beautify herself, neither did she have any desire to beautify herself, but her Bridegroom undertook that he would beautify her with salvation. As we were singing in the psalm, he beautified her by preparing a garment for her—a garment wrought with needlework, a garment in which every stitch was wrought by himself, for this was a garment that none could prepare but himself alone. That garment we call the garment of Christ's righteousness, and that garment was prepared by him in love.

1. The garment of Christ's righteousness prepared to beautify his Bride
2. Her inward beauty through the work of the Holy Spirit in her soul
3. His admiration of her beauty in her conduct

1. The garment of Christ's righteousness prepared to beautify his Bride
Let us begin then by considering the garment that Christ prepared for his Bride. This is the garment that she will wear throughout the endless ages of eternity. It is the wedding garment provided by the Bridegroom himself. That wedding garment was provided in such a way that the one who was in the kingdom of Satan would be translated to his own kingdom—the kingdom of God's dear Son, the kingdom of God's love.

When the Bridegroom prepared and worked out the needlework of this garment, he was manifesting his love to her, and his love to his Father. We read that when he was coming into the world, the Saviour said, 'To do thy will I take delight, / O thou my God that art; / Yea, that most holy law of thine / I have within my heart' (Psalm 40:8). When God the Father views the Bridegroom, he sees him not only as his beloved Son—not only as his own divine image and his uncreated fullness—not only as the outshining of his glory through his divine person—but also he sees him in his glory as the Father's Servant. He who was the Son of God became the Servant of the

Father in order that he would, as the Bridegroom, prepare a garment for his Bride. So the Father sees him in the glory of his being the Father's Servant, carrying out the work of providing for this Bride a garment that she would wear throughout the endless ages of eternity.

In connection with the preparation of that garment, we see that what was required of the Bridegroom was obedience. Obedience was required of the first Adam under the covenant of works—he was required to fulfil that covenant by obedience. It was something Adam was quite capable of doing, and by that obedience his seed would have been partakers of the life that shall never end. The covenant of works was based on the obedience of Adam, but Adam failed. He fell by his sin, and we fell in him, and that arrangement is gone forever. It is impossible for us now to give the obedience that Adam should have given, and therefore we, like him, are now the children of wrath. But now, in the fullness of time, the Bridegroom came, and he came to be obedient.

I want to stress that point: he was being obedient. It was in obedience to his Father that he prepared this garment, without which his Bride could not come out of the kingdom of darkness—without which his Bride could never be the Prince's daughter. The nature of Christ's obedience is brought before us by the apostle in writing to the Ephesians when he says, 'Walk in love, as Christ also loved us.' Christ's obedience was a walking in love. It was a walking in love from the womb of his mother, where he took into union with his divine person the holy humanity conceived by the power of the Holy Ghost, in that womb in which man never lay before. When the Saviour died he was buried in a grave wherein man was never laid before, and when he was born, he came from a womb in which man had never lain before. The power of the Holy Ghost over-shadowed Mary, sanctifying and setting apart of her substance, cleansing it from all sin. By his divine power he conceived a holy humanity, body and soul, of her substance, the Son of God.

He was the Bridegroom of the Church by a personal act of his own, done in love to his Father. 'A body hast thou prepared for me,' he said in love to his Father when he took the humanity into union with his divinity. It was also done in love to his people. This is what he was saying when he took the holy human nature into union with his divine person—this is bone of my bone and flesh of my flesh, this is the nature of my Bride whom I love. He took it into union with his divine person and then from the womb of his mother he began to walk in love. Because he was born of a woman, therefore he was made under the law, as we read (Galatians 4:4), so that when he walks in love he was engaged in satisfying the claim of the law with regard to obedience. It was the obedience not of a mere man, or of a perfect man, or even of a sinless man anointed by the Holy Spirit with all the graces appropriate to an innocent holy human nature—but it was the obedience of the Son of God in your nature and mine. In this way the law was magnified and made honourable.

The law was made honourable by this person walking in love, but then he had to be obedient even unto death. Paul says, 'Walk in love, as Christ also hath loved us, and *hath given himself for us an offering and a sacrifice* to God for a sweet-smelling savour' (Ephesians 5:2). From his mother's womb, he walked in love, and every step he took was a step in love to his Bride. O the glory of his Father! Every step was taking him to the cross of Calvary. Every step was taking him to that time when he would lovingly and freely offer himself a sacrifice to satisfy divine justice on behalf of the sins of all the members of the Bride whom he loved with an everlasting love and for whom he was providing this garment. This garment that we call the garment of Christ's righteousness consists first of all in his obedience to the law of God and secondly in his obedience unto death.

His sacrifice of himself was a sweet smelling savour to God. Now you remember when Noah came out of the ark after the Flood, he built an altar. When he offered a sacrifice on the altar, we read that God smelled a sweet savour (Genesis 8:21). The Hebrew words there mean a savour of rest. That was just a type, a foreshadowing, but when we come to the cross of Calvary, we come to the fulfilment of the type. When this person died in the room and place of the guilty, bearing the sins of his own people in his own body upon the tree, there was a savour from that sacrifice. It was a savour in which

God the everlasting Father smelled a savour of rest. The claims of his holy law found rest. The claims of his justice found rest. His divine nature and his claims upon his people found rest in the death and the sacrifice of the Saviour. It was a savour that filled all the attributes of God, and he rested, and rested in his love. This was the garment that the Bridegroom prepared, so that she who was in the kingdom of Satan, serving diverse lusts and pleasures, would be clothed with this garment and would come to be called (as she is here) the Prince's daughter. She had a garment worthy of the Prince's daughter. Though unworthy in herself, the garment made her worthy to be the Bride of the Son of God.

She began to wear the garment in this world. Now she had a garment to cover her nakedness, a garment to make her acceptable to God, a garment through which she was justified by faith, a garment through which she obtained the forgiveness of sins according to the riches of God's grace: when she came to be clothed with it, being justified by faith, she had peace with God, through her Bridegroom.

2. Her inward beauty through the work of the Holy Spirit in her soul

We will then go on to consider in the second place that she also needed an inward beauty, which is given to her by the work of the Holy Spirit in her soul. You see, something took place in the soul, in the inward heart of this person who was brought into the Father's house. Those people who are now in the Father's house had previously been in the kingdom of Satan, serving diverse lusts and pleasures, but they came to experience in their souls something that brought them out of that kingdom.

What brought them out of this kingdom was the call of the Bridegroom. 'O daughter, hearken and regard, / and do thine ear incline; / Likewise forget thy father's house, / and people that are thine' (Psalm 45:10). 'Let the wicked forsake his way, and the unrighteous man his thoughts: and let him return unto the Lord, and he will have mercy upon him; and to our God, for he will abundantly pardon' (Isaiah 55:7). The voice of Christ was heard in the soul, in the darkness of Satan's kingdom along with her companions of darkness.

It was a call to come out of that kingdom. It was a call to forsake the foolish and live. It was a call to forget her father's house and turn her back on the companions that she had there, who worked together to ripen each other for a lost eternity. Now this voice broke in upon her soul and said, 'Incline thine ear, and come unto me.'

So when the Holy Spirit applied the Word of God to the soul, the soul discovered that he or she was in the kingdom of Satan, in the kingdom of darkness, on the broad way to everlasting destruction. It was the same as when Lazarus was lying in the grave. There he was, in the darkness and coldness of the grave, but then he heard the voice of the Son of God, saying, 'Lazarus, come forth!' In the moment that he was quickened, he discovered himself in the grave. So it is with all those who have heard the voice of Christ by the power of the Holy Ghost in their soul's experience. They came to discover they were in the kingdom of darkness. They came to discover they were among the enemies of God. They came to discover that their sins were more than could be numbered. They came to realise that if they were going to stay there then there was nothing for them but that they would perish, according to the Word of God—the wages of sin is death. But now they heard the voice of the Saviour, and he was saying to them, 'Incline your ear'—come away from the allurements of the world, come away from the pleasures of the world, and incline your ear instead to the gospel of the grace of God.

Incline your ear to the glorious gospel of the grace of God! Incline your ear to hear the gospel trumpet, declaring, 'Whosoever will, let him take of the water of life freely!' Listen to the gospel trumpet, declaring that the Son of man is come to seek and to save that which was lost! Listen to the gospel telling the soul about the Bridegroom of the Church, and rejoice, as John the Baptist said, to hear the Bridegroom's voice! In their soul's experience, sinners come to understand their need of the gospel—their need of heeding the gospel—their need of inclining their ears to the gospel. Now they incline their ears to the gospel to see if there is anything in Christ for them. Now they listen in order that they would arrive at a conclusion about Christ. Now they find that they must enquire why Christ came into the world, and they listen for the answer, given by Paul, by the inspiration of the Holy Spirit: 'This is a faithful saying, and worthy of all acceptation, that Christ Jesus came into the world *to save sinners.*'

Now, did that ever become the gospel to you? Did it become good news to you that Christ came into the world to save sinners? He came to save sinners who cannot save themselves—to save sinners who cannot do anything to deliver themselves. *In him* there is a righteousness, a salvation. The garments of salvation are in *Christ*, and Christ can clothe the soul with the garments of salvation. The soul comes to understand and to see in the light of the Word of God the way that a sinner comes. The soul comes as a lost sinner, a guilty sinner, a ruined sinner, a sinner who has no help of man at all—a sinner who is saying, 'I looked on my right hand and viewed, / but none to know me were; / All refuge failed me, no man / did for my soul take care' (Psalm 142:4). So what then do they say? 'I cried to thee; I said, Thou art / my refuge, Lord, alone; / And in the land of those that live / thou art my portion' (verse 5). Thou art my portion! That's the exercise of faith, going out to Christ in the gospel. They come to understand that it is through believing on Christ that a soul comes to be clothed with the garment of righteousness. It is through believing on Christ that a soul comes to be clothed with the garments of salvation.

This garment appears very precious to them when they view the Saviour. They view the Saviour's obedience to the law of God, his obedience unto death, and they realise that it was something they didn't love before. 'Walk in love,' says Paul to the Ephesians. 'Walk in love, as Christ also hath loved us.' Every step that Christ took, from the womb of his mother to the cross of Calvary, he did it all in love. When he died on the cross and said 'It is finished,' the robe was then complete. The righteousness of Christ needs nothing to be added to it—no circumcision, no works of their own of any kind or description. It is a complete robe to beautify the Bride. On account of the robe of Christ's righteousness, the Bride—she who had been in the kingdom of darkness, guilty, corrupt, undone—she is called the Prince's daughter. It was in union to the Prince of Peace, the Solomon of the New

Testament, that she could come to be clothed in this garment. In other words, it was through being espoused to the Saviour (and that by faith of the operation of God) that she came to wear this garment. Christ's righteousness was imputed to her by God the Father upon her believing in Christ.

Now the soul comes to see and understand that. The great concern of the soul came to be, 'O that I knew where I might find him!' (Job 23:3). Coming to the house of God they were saying, 'Sir, we would see Jesus' (John 12:21). They were pleading that the Holy Spirit would take of the things of Christ and reveal them to their souls, so that they would be enabled to believe in him and enabled to embrace him, enabled to rest in him alone for salvation. This took place in the experience of every member of the Bride of Christ. Each of them came to this experience, of resting in Christ alone for salvation.

And they came to that experience when, as the Saviour says in regard to another, 'he had nothing to pay.' They gave up every attempt to pay. All this attempt to produce some merit of their own was now completely gone. The soul comes now to rest in Christ, and to rest in him alone for salvation. That is what faith is. Faith is a grace of the Holy Spirit, but faith in exercise is a resting in Christ as the Saviour. He spoke to the Jews of the will of his Father, that sinners would 'see the Son and believe on him' (John 6:40). And so faith is a spiritual viewing of Christ, to the effect that you believe in him, that you trust in him for salvation. It is such a view of Christ that you feel a drawing in your soul to rest in him and to believe in him for salvation. This is what faith is—a resting in Christ and believing in him and trusting in him and depending upon him. As Paul said (2 Timothy 1:12), the Lord was 'able to keep that which I have committed to him'. And what was that? It was his guilty soul, a soul lost in itself, and Paul in the exercise of faith committed his soul to Christ for his soul to be clothed, for his soul to be saved with an everlasting salvation.

So it is in the spiritual experience of God's people: they come to trust in the Saviour and to lean upon him and trust in him for salvation. When that takes place, then, as we read, 'being justified by faith, we have peace with God through our Lord Jesus Christ' (Romans 5:1). When the soul is wearing the wedding garment of the righteousness of Christ, the first benefit of all is the forgiveness of sins. God sees the Prince's daughter wearing the garment the Bridegroom has given her. God sees the sinner clothed in the righteousness of Christ. So God says with regard to that soul, 'His or her sins and iniquities I will remember no more for ever.' They are accepted into God's favour—being justified by faith, they have peace with God.

Think of the mode in which the sinner casts a look of faith to Christ and trusts in him for salvation. They look to him alone, according to his word, 'Look unto me, and be ye saved, all the ends of the earth' (Isaiah 45:22). The sinner is at the ends of the earth in his spiritual experience, and ready to fall over into a lost eternity. They feel just like the thief on the cross—was he not at the ends of earth, was he not just ready to fall into a lost eternity? And what happened? He cast the look of faith to Christ: 'Lord, remember me when thou comest into thy kingdom' (Luke 23:42)—and he hung his hope for eternity on Christ and him crucified. Therefore, according to the Word of God, none perish—you among them—*none* perish that him trust. None perish that him trust! (Psalm 34:22) That garment on the soul can never be taken away. That garment remains on the soul throughout the endless ages of eternity. We read in the Word of God that Abraham believed God and it was counted unto him for righteousness. The moment he was justified, that moment the righteousness of Christ became his. He has now been made perfect in holiness and has been for thousands of years in everlasting glory, but that's the garment he wore, the garment that was given to him the moment that he believed on Christ, and that is the garment he is still wearing now. It is the same garment that all the Lord's people wear. Although they themselves feel cast down on many occasions because of their darkness, because of their sins and their iniquities, yet the Bridegroom sees them clothed in the garment of this righteousness, and therefore he calls her a Prince's daughter.

The next point is that a work is now begun in their souls which is to be carried on until the day of Jesus Christ. In other words, in their effectual calling, a principle of holiness is imparted to the soul, or we may call it a principle of spiritual life. We read in the Word of God that those who belong to the Bride of Christ are partakers of the divine nature. Now of course that does not mean that they are partakers of the divine essence, because that is incommunicable—infinite, eternal, and unchangeable. But it does mean that in the moment of regeneration, the Holy Spirit imparts to the soul by his gracious power a new nature, a holy nature. In the moment of regeneration, a godly nature is imparted to the soul, and that nature begins to have its exercises in the graces of the Holy Spirit.

Regeneration is the Holy Spirit laying—not new faculties, but a new nature, or, if you like the word, a new foundation in the soul. This means that the faculties of the soul are exercised in a different way from when they were unregenerate. The understanding now delights in the Word of God—'I did find thy words and I did eat them, and they became the joy and rejoicing of my heart.' The conscience rests in the blood of Christ, and flees to the blood of Christ. 'I flee to thee to cover me' (Psalm 143:9). I flee to the Bridegroom's blood to cover me. Also the affections move out in love to Christ—'I love the Lord, because my voice / and prayers he did hear' (Psalm 116:1).

These exercises are all now taking place in the soul and the Saviour, the Bridegroom, sees them, and he knows this is the work of the Spirit of God. He knows these exercises are there because that soul was purchased with his own precious blood. And because that soul is a member of his Bride, therefore he delights in their faith's exercises. He delights in their godly sorrow for sin. He delights in the hope that they have, for they have the hope that they will be with Christ himself one day. When they were justified by faith they had peace with God through the Lord Jesus Christ and came to rejoice—in what?—in the hope of the glory of God. The Saviour sees in the exercises of the Holy Spirit that which dignifies the people of God, placing them above and apart from the world and all the dignities and dignitaries of the world. When he looks on the people of the world, he sees nothing but vanity. But when he sees a soul where faith is trembling, where hope is aspiring, where the soul is waiting upon himself, where there is a longing and a thirsting for himself, what does he see there? He sees there a beauty, and it is the beauty of the Prince's daughter, the beauty of the Bride of Christ.

That beauty is to continue for ever. As we read, 'he will beautify the meek with salvation' (Psalm 149:4). It is a beauty that will continue until the work is done, and at death the soul will be made perfect in holiness and will go into the presence of God. After time is over and the body is raised from the dead, the Bride of Christ will be brought by him to the Father—behold I and the children thou hast given me, I and the bride that thou hast given me. She will be without blemish and without spot and without wrinkle. She will be perfectly beautified. At last when she is in everlasting glory going in to the marriage supper of the Lamb, she will be without blemish and without spot, and even without wrinkle—no sign even of age, because in her soul is the life that shall never end—just as the Saviour's locks are bushy, and black as a raven (Song 5:11)—no grey hairs. Christ will never grow old, and his love will never grow cold. And here is his Bride, and she will never grow old, and, wonder of wonders, her love will never grow cold—no, not throughout the endless ages of eternity. She will be made perfect, and because of this inward beauty, she is all glorious within.

3. His admiration of her beauty in her conduct

In the third place we will consider what is in these words—the particular feature of her beauty which he mentions here: 'How beautiful are thy feet with shoes, O prince's daughter!' He saw not only the beauty in her garment—and, yes of course he saw something of the beauty of the inward work of the Holy Ghost in her heart—but he is also referring here to this beauty that he sees in her, 'her feet with shoes'. When he sees this beauty he rejoices, and he loves her, and this draws out his love to her.

This is a reference to the walk of the people of God. They have shoes for their walk. We read in Ephesians that when believers put on the whole armour of God, their feet are shod with the preparation of the gospel of peace. When the Saviour sees this, he says, 'How beautiful are thy feet with shoes, O prince's daughter!' This marks her out with the dignity of being the Prince's daughter, the fact that her feet are shod with the preparation of the gospel of peace.

Now this means first of all that she walks in communion and fellowship with her Bridegroom, who is the Prince of Peace. She walks in the light of that truth. She is walking in the light of the gospel. She is enjoying fellowship with the Prince of Peace and she walks in such a way that she may enjoy that fellowship. She walks in the light as he is in the light, that she may have fellowship with him. And when she has fellowship with him, what does she enjoy? 'Thou wilt keep him in perfect peace, whose mind is stayed on thee: because he trusteth in thee' (Isaiah 26:3). The soul that has fellowship with the Prince of Peace is a soul that enjoys a peace of soul which passes all understanding—a peace that they cannot put into words, the peace that they enjoy when they get nearness of soul to Christ, and fellowship with Christ in the gospel.

This also reminds us of the footsteps of the flock. When the feet of a soul are shod with the preparation of the gospel of peace, they follow the footsteps of the flock—they are found where the people of God are. They go forth by the shepherd's steps, they love the counsel of peace, they love the house of God. 'The habitation of thy house, / Lord, I have loved well' (Psalm 26:8). That's the direction their feet go. Here they are, and do you hear them singing as their feet are shod with the preparation of the gospel of peace, 'I joyed when to the house of God, / go up they said to me. / Jerusalem, within thy gates / my feet shall standing be'? Their walk is towards the house of God and their delight is in the house of God and in the people of God.

And all they do is shot through with obedience. Their steps are the steps of obedience. They are the steps of obedience to Christ, obedience to the Word of God, obedience to the word of truth. This characterises and dignifies the people of God. Those who live in the world are living in opposition to God. They turn their feet away from God's commands, away from the gospel, away from the means of grace. But the Prince's daughter, her feet are clothed with the preparation of the gospel of peace and she walks in the way of God's commandments. They are obedient. Obedience is something which the Word of God requires of a wife. If that is true of the natural marriage, then how much more is it true of the spiritual marriage—that the Bride of Christ would be obedient to her husband. When she walks in obedience, then this is what he says, 'How beautiful are thy feet with shoes, O prince's daughter!'

This is what he says when she is walking in the paths of obedience. This is what he says when she is saying, 'Great peace have they who love thy law; / offence they shall have none' (Psalm 119:165). He sees her beauty when she delights in having her feet in the paths of righteousness. Indeed the Lord's people pray for that—not only to enjoy the peace by the still waters, as the psalmist says in Psalm 23, but also that the Lord would guide their feet in the paths of righteousness, even for his own name's sake. David is saying there that if he was to depart from the paths of righteousness, as someone one who had the name of God on him, then the name of God would be dishonoured. So the shoes are worn in the obedience which the people of God render to the Prince of Peace. They desire to obey him, and they do render obedience to him, because of what he did for them, and because they have in their souls a desire to have communion and fellowship with him.

The Saviour sees the beauty in that. The world does not see any beauty in that at all, but Christ does. Here is a man, here is a woman, and here's a young person, and Christ has been made precious to him and to her, and they are distinguished by the fact that their walk and life and conversation are conformed to the Word of God (and that through their minds being transformed, as Paul says). That's the way they are and that's why they come to hear the Word of God preached—to get fresh light upon the truth and so that their minds would be renewed and so that they would grow in grace and in the knowledge of their Lord and Saviour Jesus Christ.

Now the Prince of Peace has instituted in this world a particular place where he will meet with his Bride. First he said, 'With desire I have desired to eat this passover with you before I suffer,' (Luke 22:15) and then he laid the passover aside and introduced the Lord's Supper into the Church of God by his own divine blessed authority. There he says to his people—yes, to the Prince's daughter—he says, 'Take, eat: this is my body that was broken for you,' and, 'This cup is the new testament in my blood; this do ye as oft as ye drink it, in remembrance of me.'

Now this is a command from the Prince of Peace, and those who are spiritually taught by the Word of God come to understand that this is part of the preparation of the gospel of peace. This feast is prepared for them by the Prince of Peace, so that they might be fed, so that they might be strengthened. It is a place where they can be obedient to him and honour him and witness on his side. All the Lord's people here who will be sitting at the Lord's table tomorrow will be witnessing to the rest of the people in this building that this is how they are related to the Prince of Peace: 'This is my beloved, and this is my friend, O daughters of Jerusalem.'

Of course the Lord's people may feel their unworthiness, and on many occasions they do feel they are coming short with regard to this ordinance. But the fact remains that they must be obedient to Christ in it. So there comes a time that whatever doubts, fears, tremblings, and hesitations the soul may have, yet this command, 'This do in remembrance of me', becomes something that the soul cannot overlook any longer—they are bound by the grace of God to be obedient to it. When that takes place, then the Saviour sees a beauty in it. He sees a spiritual beauty in that obedience. 'How beautiful are thy feet with shoes, O prince's daughter!'

He sees their beauty. He speaks to this soul and that soul, calling them 'Prince's daughter'. That is what we call the sealing nature of the Lord's supper—he confirms to them that they belong to his people, to the living church of God. When the soul takes a piece of the bread and a sip of the wine, and does so looking by faith to Christ, then Christ is sealing to that soul that he or she belongs Christ's people—they are the Prince's daughter. Christ is saying to that soul, 'Thou art mine.' Thou art mine! As the soul is feeding by faith upon Christ in the Lord's supper, Christ is seeing a beauty in that and is calling that soul 'Prince's daughter' and expressing his love for her. 'How beautiful are thy feet with shoes, O prince's daughter!'

May he bless his Word. Let us call upon his name.

11 Brethren dwelling in unity

PSALM 133

A song of degrees of David

Behold, how good and how pleasant it is for brethren to dwell
together in unity! It is like the precious ointment upon the head,
that ran down upon the beard, even Aaron's beard: that went down
to the skirts of his garments; as the dew of Hermon, and as the
dew that descended upon the mountains of Zion: for there the Lord
commanded the blessing, even life for evermore.

ACTION SERMON ON LORD'S DAY, INVERNESS COMMUNION,
30TH JANUARY 2000

This psalm is a song of degrees, bound up with the tribes of Israel going up to Jerusalem to render thanks to God for his testimony. It must have been a wonderful sight to see these tribes gathering in from all ends of the Promised Land, making their way in unity to keep the feast that God had appointed should be kept by them, bound up with the testimony of God in their midst. No doubt as the Psalmist wrote this Psalm he was seeing the gathering of the tribes from all corners—the tribe of Judah, the tribe of little Benjamin, the tribe of Ephraim, and all the people in the tribes. They were going up in unity to worship God with respect to the Passover, to keep in remembrance the wonderful deliverance he had given them, when he brought them out of the land of Egypt by the blood of the Paschal Lamb and the power of the Holy Ghost.

1. We shall enquire first of all with regard to the brethren who are spoken of here. They are all members of the human family. The sheep of Christ are the children of men, not angels or archangels or cherubims or seraphims. 'The flock of my pasture,' says Ezekiel, speaking on behalf of the Lord (Ezekiel 34:31), 'are men.' Therefore we shall begin by taking a view of the children of men dwelling in unity the sense that we are all one in Adam. This unity embraces you, and it embraces me, and it embraces every member of the human race: they dwelt in unity in Adam as the federal head of the human race. Adam was indeed the root of mankind, that is true, but when God took steps by a special act of his providence after he had created man, he entered into covenant with Adam, and constituted Adam the federal head of that covenant. By the expression 'the federal head' we mean that the covenant embraced not only Adam himself, but the whole human race in him. By the decree of God, the whole human race were constituted to be united in him and united to him.

2. Secondly we shall take a view of this unity in their being embraced by the love of God the Father. They were all embraced by that love, they all dwell in that love. Moses said this in Psalm 90, 'Lord, thou hast been our dwelling-place in generations all'—yes, and even in eternity. There were those of the human race who dwelt in the love of God the Father, and therefore we shall enquire (as the Lord may enable) into this great and wonderful matter. Every one of them, the small and great in this world, were all embraced in the eternal love of God the Father—they had a unity in the bosom of the Father's love before the world was.

3. Then in the third place we shall go on to notice their unity in their High Priest. That is brought before us beautifully in this Psalm. Of course, all the Word of God is beautiful—all the revelations of the Word of God have a beauty and a glory that are incomparable. It cannot be seen in any other way but as an excellent glory. We find a reference here to Aaron the High Priest, and on the day of atonement, as Aaron appeared before God, the whole of Israel were in unity in him. He appeared before God on their behalf, and

33

he appeared alone on their behalf. The day of atonement was the great day when the unity of Israel was seen in their being all united in the High Priest.

4. Then, in the fourth and last place, we should like to enquire into the unity of the brethren in the Holy Ghost. Now we'll come to explain, if we are able to do so and are given grace to do so, that what we are to understand by the oil on Aaron's head and the dew of Hermon is the unity of the people of God in God the Holy Ghost. God's people have a unity in the Holy Ghost, and that unity is bound up with the Lord's Supper, for when the people of God appear at the Lord's Table to remember the death of Christ, they are appearing there in unity. There they are manifesting not only their hope of union to Christ and their union to Christ and their profession with regard to Christ ('this is my beloved, and this is my friend') but also they are saying with regard to the others at the table, 'These are my friends and my brethren, these are my brothers and sisters.' The unity at the Lord's table is unity in the dew of Hermon.

Now these truths, if we were able to explain them even to some extent, have a beauty and glory that the world knows nothing of. There is plenty of talk about union, church union, union of nations, and so on, and it is mere empty worthless words: but here we have a wonderful unity, a glorious unity, a unity that will not come to an end even at death. It is a unity over which death has no power. Not even death will separate the people of God from Christ, and death will not eventually separate the people of God from one another. They are united to one another in the dew of Hermon, in the oil of the Holy Ghost, and as they are together at the Lord's Table in time, so they will be together at the marriage supper of the Lamb throughout the endless ages of eternity.

Those of you here, young men and young women as well as others, take note of the fact that what you are to see today with the eye of your bodies is pointing forward to the marriage supper of the Lamb. At the marriage supper of the Lamb, Christ will be there, alive for ever more. The Church said that the locks of Christ were black as a raven—there were no grey hairs. There were grey hairs in Ephraim but not on the head of the Saviour, for he shall never die again. He is alive, and alive for evermore, and his love will never grow cold. More wonderful still, those who are united in the dew of Hermon, they will never grow old either, there will be no wrinkles or any such thing. They have what we are told of here, 'the blessing God commands, life that shall never end'—life united to Christ and life united to his people.

1. The unity of mankind

But we must begin, if we are to understand things, with the whole human race being united in Adam. Now you see, the modern pseudo-Christianity knows nothing about this. You won't hear about this if you read the theological books by people who call themselves theologians and call one another theologians—this great fact of the unity of the human race in Adam. The unity of the human race in Adam is not just that Adam is the root or father of the human race. That is true, but the unity I am referring to here is a unity with regard to a special act of God's providence. These are the words of the Catechism (and you should pay close attention to the words of the Catechism), 'a special act of God's providence'.

Now there was no necessity for God to create the world. There was no necessity in the divine nature for God to create the world: it was an act of a decree in accordance with his purpose to manifest and make known his glory. There was no necessity, for God is perfectly blessed in himself. He is perfectly blessed in the love of the Father and the love of the Son and the love of the Holy Ghost. God is perfectly blessed in the communion of eternal love, and he does not need anything to be added to make him, as it were, more blessed. He is blessed in himself.

Therefore when he created the world it was a sovereign act, it was something in accordance with his divine mind to reveal his glory and his power. He sovereignly chose to reveal the glory of his power and the glory of his wisdom in creating the world. And as he created the world for this purpose, so he created spiritual beings that they might perceive that glory. And these spiritual beings we call angels. Because they were spiritual beings they were able to discern glory of God and the image of God shining in the created universe. They sang for joy. This was a spiritual song by the myriads, the thousands upon thousands, of the angelic host. They sang together about the glory of God revealed in creation.

Then it pleased God to create man, and this was a wonderful thing. It must have been one of the things that the angels desired to look into in connection with creation. Here was God whom they knew to be a pure spirit, and here he was creating a creature, which first of all had a body made from the earth. This creature had a body made from the earth, and then the Spirit of God breathed into him, and when that took place, man became a living soul. We read also that this was a result of the communion and fellowship of the three Persons within the Godhead. They said, 'Let us make man in our image' (Genesis 1:26). So here he was, this creature of God, body and soul—heaven and earth meeting in him, in a way that it did not meet even in the angels. The angels had no bodies, but here was a creature, man, created by God with a body and with a soul, a soul from heaven and a body from the earth. A wonderful creature, a unique creature among all the other realms of creatures, in which heaven and earth met together.

And God had a peculiar pleasure and delight in him. He placed him in a garden and the garden was called Eden, which as you know means delight. It was a garden of delight, for one thing because, when Adam looked round that garden in his state of innocence, he could view the goodness of God on the right hand and on the left, and in the sun and moon and stars. But also it was a garden of delight because it was a garden where God came in the cool of the day. In other words it was a place in which Adam had fellowship with God, and God had fellowship with Adam.

Now, just in passing, you see that one of the effects of the evolutionary hypothesis is to strike a blow at the uniqueness of man, when it asserts that man comes from, or develops, through various phases, from other creatures. The sense of the uniqueness of man is being lost, both in universities and in schools, even though it is only a hypothesis which hasn't been proved (and can't be proved). And consequently the value of life has decreased in our day, and even murder has become common. This all springs from a lack of the proper view of the uniqueness of man in his creation at the beginning.

But we see now this taking place, a special act of God's providence. God entered into a covenant with man. There were the angels—myriads of them—glorious beings, who sang with joy at the creation of the universe. But God did not make this particular act of divine providence towards angels. Instead it was toward man, manifesting the peculiar delight that God had in man. He entered into a covenant with man. That covenant depended upon man's obedience and would have been a covenant of life if Adam had not disobeyed. When Adam was created he had *spiritual* life in his soul, but in order that he might have *eternal* life, according to the administration of God, he would need to have a course of obedience. The principle of obtaining life by creatures is this, that 'the man which doeth those things shall live by them' (Romans 10:5), or in other words, the man who does the will of God will obtain life by that will. Therefore, in order that Adam would have eternal life, it was necessary for him to have a period of obedience in which he would have, not just the righteousness of his nature, but a righteousness that would entitle him to life.

This was the covenant that God made with man and this is what I want to emphasise now. We're taking a view of Adam now and the whole human race in him, as he was constituted by God as the federal head of the human race. In this covenant the whole human race are in him. You and I were there when the covenant was made—we were there in Adam, because he was the federal head. Adam was equipped with all the qualifications necessary to fulfil the terms of the covenant which were, in essence, to obey the will of God. And a test was put upon him, that he would not eat of the fruit of the tree of the knowledge of good and evil. So the promise of life was there, life that shall never end.

What a delightsome garden it was indeed, when God made that covenant with Adam! The delight in the garden was more delightful than before, because manifested here was a special act of God's providence towards man. So this is the first place where we have to look when we consider this unity. This is what the unity of the human race consists in: every member of the human race, whether they are Jews, Muslims, Buddhists, and so on, were all in Adam when God entered into this covenant with him. They were in him and they were united in him.

But Adam fell. He fell by the temptation of Satan, an angel who had sung with joy. Yes, Satan and the others who came to be in the rebellion which he led, they all sang with joy on the morning of the creation. But they moved out of their place—they aspired to be higher than where God had set them in creation. Once that happened and pride took hold in them, then they were cast out of heaven and reserved in chains of darkness till the judgment of the great day (2 Peter 2:4).

Now, into Eden, and into this delightsome garden, came this dark spirit, and he tempted Adam with the very temptation by which he fell himself. 'Ye shall be as gods, knowing good and evil.' When Adam then took of the fruit of the tree of the knowledge of good and evil, the whole human race fell in him. They had been brethren in the sense that they were created by God, all the sons of Adam, but now they became united as the children of wrath. The sentence of death passed upon Adam was passed upon them in him. Adam was driven out of the garden, and the fiery sword of divine justice moving from one side to another was put in place to guard the way to the tree of life. And when Adam was put outside, so was the whole human family in him. So were you and so was I. We were all expelled from the favour of God. We see them now as the children of wrath by reason of the fall in their first covenant head. They are united as the children of wrath, under the sentence of death and ready to perish.

2. The unity of God's chosen people

And yet the Word of God brings before us another unity. And what a wonderful unity it is. It is a unity in these words, 'I have loved thee with an everlasting love.' The Word of God brings before us the great and wonderful fact that a number that no man can number of the human race were embraced in the love of God the Father. He united them in electing them to eternal life and loving them.

Now, let us pause here again to remember this, that when God purposed to bring many sons to glory, there was no need in God for that to happen. That was the effect of this love that embraced them from all eternity: it was to bring them, as many sons, to glory (Hebrews 2:10). But there was no need in God for that to take place. You see the doctrine of the Universal Fatherhood of God is based upon an assumption that since God is a Father he must have children. And therefore (the argument goes on to say) the whole human race are the family of God and therefore of course God would not punish them on account of their sins, and furthermore they are not really the children of wrath because there is no wrath in the Father.

That is what they teach, but where they principally go astray is that they lose sight of the fact there was no necessity in God the Father to have many sons to bring to glory. He already had one Son, and that Son was the Son of his love, the second person of the Godhead. He was *the* object of the Father's love, the peculiar object of the love of the Father. The Father's love was going out to him and the Son's love was going out to the Father and both in the communion of the Spirit of love, the Holy Ghost. God the Father's love—his everlasting, eternal, infinite love—was completely satisfied with the object of his love, that is, his beloved Son, the brightness of his glory, the express image of his Person (Hebrews 1:3). So here again we have a sovereign act of God, in his love going out and in the purpose of his love, to bring 'many sons to glory'.

Now we believe it to be true of Satan when he caused man to fall, that if it was possible for that dark spirit to have any sense of pleasure, this is what he was pleased about. First of all he rejoiced that Adam had lost God—he had lost the favour of God, he was a lost soul. Adam's destiny, Satan was quite sure, was to be with himself and the other fallen angels in hell throughout the endless ages of eternity. But also he rejoiced that God had lost Adam. God had lost man—that is what he thought. But he did not know the mind of the Lord. Satan had no perception of the eternal counsels of Jehovah. And he had no conception of the fact that God had loved a number that no man can number of the lost and ruined human race, and that he loved them in a sovereign and merciful and gracious way, and that he purposed to bring many sons to glory from among the children of men.

Now, that did not apply to the angels who fell. Satan was quite sure that the justice of God would require that Adam would be punished with himself, and that's what Satan is after still. It is still his desire, and the whole ingenuity and exercises of the power of his kingdom are towards this end, to have members of the human race with him, with the devil and his angels. That's his purpose. That's why there are cinemas and dances and television shows of one kind and another. That's why the whole world of entertainment exists, that vast vile cesspool of moral filth, to ensure that men and woman will forget their souls, and go on enjoying the pleasures of sin which are but for a season, and then on the other side of death, they'll be with the devil and his angels. Christ will say on the day of judgment to those who have despised him and despised his gospel, 'Depart from me, ye cursed, into everlasting fire, prepared for the devil and his angels' (Matthew 25:41).

Are you here today who despise Christ? Are you here who despise him in the sense that you will not have him, you will not receive him, you will not believe in him, you will not flee to him for the salvation of your soul? Then that is your destiny as long as you continue in that way. But here we have this wonderful unity of this people embraced by the love of God the Father! This is what caused the Psalmist to plead, 'Remember me, Lord, with that love' (Psalm 106:4). Will you not yourself join in that prayer today, when I'm speaking about the love of the Father? Will you not consider the unity of the people of God in that love—every one of them loved, every one loved separately and every one loved also together, loved as the many sons that are to be brought to glory? Will you not therefore this Sabbath morning—will you not, oh will you not pray this prayer and cry, 'Remember me, Lord, with that love / which thou to thine dost bear; / With thy salvation, O my God, / to visit me draw near'?

But now, how are they to come to enjoy the love of the Father? How are they to come to enjoy the love of God? Between the tree of life and the human race is the sword of God aflame with the fire of holy wrath, and those who are loved by God are among the members of the human race. They too are excluded from the tree of life by the sword turning this way and that way, and the cherubim of glory there to show that the throne of God was behind that sword. And the throne of God might crack and the universe go out of existence before one sinner who dies outside of Christ will escape being laid in hell by the sword of divine justice. But how can this be? How could it be that these people who were loved from all eternity could be brought to enjoy that love when they were the children of wrath, when they were at enmity to God by wicked works, and when divine justice had condemned them to eternal death?

3. The unity in the High Priest

Well, that brings me to the next unity. Now this was shown in the days of the ceremonial law, shedding light upon what was true when the fulfilment of the ceremonies would come. The people of Israel were united in their High Priest.

There was Aaron, set apart by God through the agency of Moses to be a high priest. The function of a high priest, or any priest, was to appear before God on behalf of sinful people. Now there were many sacrifices under the ceremonial law—in the morning and the evening a lamb was slain and so on—but what we are concerned with at the present moment is the great day of atonement in Israel.

The great day of atonement in Israel. What happened? On that day, all the other priests—the Levites, the Kohathites—every form of priest was put to one side, and one individual appeared before the eye of God. That was Aaron, the high priest. Aaron stood there alone, but when he was there alone, the whole of Israel was represented by him. When he wore the robes for glory and beauty, his breastplate had the names of the twelve tribes of Israel on it, and in that sense he represented them all, each and every one of them, in a particular manner, in his intercession. He was representing them in exactly the same way on the day of atonement, although he was then clothed in the white robes of an ordinary priest, even as he exercised the office of a high priest.

Now when he appeared before God as the high priest, the whole of Israel were united in him. He was appearing before God on their behalf, and as we read in the chapter, he was appearing before God on their behalf to make reconciliation. On their behalf he made reconciliation in the only way that it could be done, and that was by the shedding of blood. For without the shedding of blood there is no remission of sin (Hebrews 9:22). Therefore certainly Aaron had to have a sacrifice and the shedding of blood with regard to his own sins, but when he went in, he took aside the veil and carried in the blood before the mercy seat. Then he sprinkled it seven times upon the mercy seat and seven times before the mercy seat, and so he was making atonement for the sins of Israel for that year.

Now when we turn away from all that is ceremonial, we turn to another High Priest. This High Priest was of the tribe of Judah, not of the tribe of Levi. This High Priest did not belong to the house of Aaron. He belonged to a different order altogether—a High Priest after the order of Melchisedek. Now when we come to view this High Priest then we must come back to the communion and fellowship between the Father and the Son and the Holy Ghost in the eternal counsels. In eternity another covenant was made that included the men and women whom the love of God embraced. We read in the Word of God that when God the Father addressed his Son, he says, 'Thou art my beloved Son.' My beloved Son. That, you see, is what we might call the language of God's love. 'Thou art my beloved Son', the only begotten Son of the Father, the eternally begotten Son of the Father, the Son of his love. And now here is this transaction taking place in the communion of the Father and the Son. A call is made to the Son by the Father, and the call is this, to institute him a High Priest after the order of Melchisedek. 'Thou art a priest for ever after the order of Melchisedek.'

So he was called, and he was called to be a High Priest with regard to those who were embraced by the love of the Father. They were certainly given to him as a gift, as he says himself, 'Thine they were, and thou gavest them me' (John 17:6). But what we are concerned about just now is this, that they were given to him so that he would represent them before God, to reconcile them to God. This High Priest was called from eternity, set apart in the eternal counsels, and called by God the Father to this office of the High Priest. He was to represent the children of men first of all, and secondly he was to make atonement by sacrifice. But this meant that something else was necessary. He would not only need to be the Son of God, but he would need to be the Son of Man. To act as a priest he would need to be clothed in a certain way. He would need to wear the clothes of a true humanity, a holy humanity.

And therefore we read in the epistle of Paul to the Hebrews that when Christ was coming into the world—and by coming into the world we mean that he's going to be born into the world, born of a woman—he was saying, 'A body thou hast prepared me' (Hebrews 10:5). He came in communion and fellowship with his Father, and we are admitted into that communion and fellowship when we hear the Son saying to the Father, 'A body thou hast prepared me.' When he was coming into the world he was looking to the Father who called him to the office of the priesthood, who called him to the office of high priest—he was looking to the Father to prepare a body for him. That body was prepared in the womb of a virgin called Mary, a womb in which man was never laid before, and the Holy Ghost, the third person of the Godhead, carried out the preparation of his body. The Father sent the Holy Spirit to overshadow the womb of the virgin, to conceive of her substance a holy humanity in her womb. The Son of God then took this humanity into union with his person by a personal act of his own. 'This is my body,' he says in the Lord's Supper, but he also said it when his body was being conceived by the power of the Holy Ghost. The Son of God said, 'This is my body, the gift of my Father, and the gift of my Father in order that I may be a High Priest for ever, after the order of Melchisedek.'

By a personal act of union of his own, he took that holy humanity into union with his divine person, and now he was a high priest, holy, harmless, undefiled, and separate from sinners (Hebrews 7:26). Holy, harmless and undefiled—yes! And as soon as he came into possession of that body, and as soon as he was born into the world from the womb of his mother, he was setting his face upon the great day of atonement.

The great day of atonement. The days of atonement passed year after year after year. Aaron died, and Eleazar took his place. And after him another, and so on. But here now we have *the* great day of atonement. What is the Saviour saying with regard to that day? Listen to him in communion with his Father as he is in the holy humanity in this world. He says this, 'Father, the hour is come' (John 17:1). The great day of atonement has come, when the High Priest must appear, and must appear alone.

You see these words, 'holy, harmless, undefiled, and separate from sinners' do not just mean that he was separate from sinners in the sense that he was holy, harmless and undefiled while they are sinners. That is true, but he was also separate from sinners as the High Priest—just like the high priest in Israel, who was separate from all the Israelites, and all the Levites, and all the priests. The high priest was alone, and so the Saviour was separate. He died, and he died alone. He was the priest, and he was also the sacrifice. 'Where is the Lamb?' Isaac asked Abraham as they went up the mount of Moriah, 'Here is the fire and here is the wood, but where is the lamb for the burnt offering?' But as the Father and the Son ascended the hill Calvary, this Son did not ask that question at all. Yes, the fire and the wood were there. Yes, the sword was there, charged with divine fire. But he himself was the Lamb. He offered himself without spot to God. He bore the guilt of their sins in his own body upon the tree.

Now, just you consider for a moment the eye of divine justice looking upon this person. The eye of divine justice has to say, in a greater way, and to a greater extent than Pilate said, 'I find no fault in this man.' 'I find no fault in Jesus Christ.' That was what divine justice had to say. 'I find no fault *in* him, but I see *on* him the guilt of the sins of his people, and therefore this is the gate through which the sword of divine justice passes to smite the Shepherd.' 'He was wounded for our transgressions, he was bruised for our iniquities: the chastisement of our peace was upon him' (Isaiah 53:5). He died the death which divine justice required him to die. And as divine justice saw in Christ the guilt of his people, he also saw in Christ all those. They were in him—they were in him in the sense that he was representing them, and therefore they died in him. The death that he died was their death, the death that they deserved. The blood that was shed had the efficacy to cleanse from all sin. They were saved in him with an everlasting salvation. The high priest in Israel sprinkled the blood before the most holy place, but of course the Saviour never entered into the holy place made with hands: he entered into heaven itself to present his blood there.

Now I do not have time to enter into that and I do not wish to digress. But what I must insist on is this, that when the high priest finished his work, that was that for that year. But next year, they needed another day of atonement. It was only the sins of that year that were atoned for, and then they needed another day of atonement. But when Christ cried on the cross, 'It is finished,' no other day of atonement is needed. It is over and done, his people are saved in him with an everlasting salvation, their sins are atoned for and the blood that he shed has the efficacy to reconcile them to God, to secure for them the life which shall never end, and to secure for them the pardon of all their sins. This day, as you come to the Lord's Table, as sure as it was true in Israel on the day of atonement, see the High Priest alone. Look round the types—Moses was a mighty man—the leaders of Judah, they were mighty men—but oh, where was the eye of the people of Israel? Every man's eye was upon the high priest. He stood alone. He stood alone, and their eye was fixed upon the high priest. Therefore, when you come to the Lord's Table, let your eye of faith be upon the High Priest, so that what happened on the mount of transfiguration would happen here on the mount of ordinances, that you would see no man save Jesus only. Jesus only! Direct your eye to this High Priest, and remember also that as he engaged in this office, as he did it in love to his Father, he also did it in love to your soul. There is love here. 'Walk in love,' says Paul to the church in Ephesus, 'as Christ also hath loved us, and hath given himself for an offering and a sacrifice to God for a sweet-smelling savour'—a savour of rest, as it was a sacrifice in which all the attributes of God found rest.

And so the work was done. The High Priest finished the work. And although his body was laid in a grave, his sacrifice was accepted by God. At the end of the journey his body was laid in a grave where man was never laid before. What a wonderful thing to think of, my dear friend! That humanity, that body that was conceived in the womb where man was never laid before, was now laid in the grave of Joseph of Arimithea, a grave in which no man had ever been laid before. But it was a grave out of which the great High Priest arose. You see when the high priest finished the work of atonement (here again, I must not digress, but I just mention this), he then put on the robes for glory and beauty again. And you remember that these robes had bells and pomegranates hanging from them, so when the people of Israel heard the bells, it was a joyful sound: it told them the atonement was over and the sacrifice had been accepted, and the high priest was still alive. That's the message of the everlasting gospel. The atonement is made, and the High Priest is alive, and he is alive for evermore, and so the joyful sound of the everlasting gospel can sound through the whole world.

4. The unity in the Holy Ghost

Now I come to speak about another unity, and that is unity in the dew of Hermon and the precious ointment. My time is going, but I would like to say one or two things about this.

First of all, we take the dew of Hermon in two ways. In one way, it reminds us of the words in the song of Moses, 'My doctrine shall drop as the rain, my speech shall distil as the dew' (Deuteronomy 32:2). In the experience of those who were loved with an everlasting love, those for whom Christ died, there comes a time when the doctrine of God's Word distils as the dew in their souls. It falls upon their souls, and in such a way as to convey life to their souls, the life that Christ secured for them. Or take it another way—it is the dew from Hermon that falls upon Mount Zion. It is the dew of the Holy Ghost, who says, 'I will be as the dew unto Israel.' The dew of the Holy Ghost falls upon Zion, and upon sinners in Zion, bringing them to know that they have sinned against heaven and before God.

Now, let me take the other illustration of unity and that is the precious ointment, the oil that flowed. There is no difficulty about what the oil means, because we all know that the oil speaks about the Holy Ghost. But you remember that the ointment was made of aloes and myrrh and cassia. All these ointments were melded together and then they were mingled with the oil, and as we have it here, the oil was poured upon Aaron's head. Now, let us think for a moment, if the oil was not used, what would have happened? The aloes, myrrh and cassia would have remained on Aaron's head—without the oil it would not have gone down to the skirts of his garments. So all the blessings of the everlasting covenant would have remained upon Christ's head, but for the oil of the Holy Spirit to convey these blessings down to his poor members. Like the woman with the issue of blood, they are saying, 'If I may but touch the hem of his garment, I shall be made whole.' That's how, as sinners, they come into union with Christ and are made partakers of all the benefits of redemption.

By the oil of the Holy Ghost they receive the blessings of justification, of sanctification, of adoption, of glorification, and all the blessings of the everlasting covenant, and this among them, the life that shall never end. Their life is hid with Christ in God. The life that was hid in Adam in the covenant of works was lost by the temptation of Satan when he brought Adam to sin, but the life that is hid with Christ in God for your soul and imparted to your soul shall never be lost. Satan cannot ruin it, and it is a life over which death has no power.

'Oh,' you say, 'but just a minute. I feel movements of spiritual death. I feel dead. Oh how dead and how dark I feel on many occasions!' That may be true, but still, that will not bring the life to an end. The life will revive. Let us look at Peter—there he denied his Saviour, sin got back to the throne of his soul, and overthrew him by the temptation of Satan, but you see, he had life over which death had no power, and so when the Saviour looked at him, then he went out, he got repentance and he wept bitterly, and so it will be with all the Lord's people. I remember the late James Mackay, Edinburgh— he and I often sat in the precentor's box there in days gone by—and he said to me on one occasion, 'You know, what we are missing today is that look that Christ gave to Peter.' The look that Christ gave to Peter brings about the godly sorrow that shall never be repented of.

But the last point for now is that they are united to one another. They are united to Christ, yes, and they are united to one another in Christ, by the dew of Hermon, by the joy of the Holy Ghost. They are united spiritually to one another, and that which is spiritual—the work of the Holy Spirit—is eternal. And this unity is eternal. That is one of the things that I often think about when I come to Inverness and other places where I used to be often as a young man and as a minister, and when I think of all the Lord's people who used to come here and how we used to be together. Kenneth Street was one place where I used to stay, and John MacAulay stayed there and Archie Robertson and all these godly men, and Charlotte Mackay, and all these godly women. Now, they were so happy together because they were there in the unity of the Spirit, which is the bond of peace. But I often think that however happy they were then, how much happier they are now. Now sin and sorrow has gone, and now they are around the throne and their eye is upon the Lamb in the midst of the throne, and they are joining in this song, 'Unto him that loved us, and washed us from our sins in his own blood' (Revelation 1:5).

What encouragement this is for the people of God! We have such an High Priest, leading us into the love of the Father. See what Paul says, 'The Lord direct your hearts into the love of God, and into the patient waiting for Christ' (2 Thessalonians 3:5). This supper here is a feast, where we are to feed upon the Priesthood of Christ, to feed upon the sacrifice of Christ, and to feed upon the love that knew no beginning and that knows no end. How he loves his own! He loved them even unto the end, and he will love them throughout the endless ages of eternity. And therefore be encouraged, those of you here whose desire is towards his name and towards the remembrance of him. Remember the unities that we have been endeavouring to bring before you here especially, and be encouraged, that your sin is atoned for, and life has been obtained for you in him, and life has been communicated to your soul by the dew of the doctrine of God's Word and the oil of the Holy Ghost.

May he bless his Word. Let us call upon his name.

Fencing of the Lord's table

We now come to the more solemn part of this service, the keeping in remembrance of the death of our great High Priest in accordance with his own command, 'This do in remembrance of me.'

This table of remembrance is also a feast. It is a feast at which Christ says to his people, 'Eat, o friends; drink, yea, drink abundantly, o my beloved.' To the eyes of the world the matter seems very simple—broken bread, poured out wine. How that would be despised by the great people of this world with their great feasts of one kind or another! But what is made known at this feast has a far greater glory. It is not the glory of the world, but a spiritual glory that we have in the bread broken and wine poured out, revealing and making known the eternal salvation of the many sons that will be brought to glory, according to the institution of the one whose body was broken and whose blood was shed.

Now since this feast is a spiritual feast, it follows that those who come to this feast are spiritual. Those who are invited to the feast on the table of the everlasting gospel are invited to come as they are, but those who come to this feast here, they are spiritual, because the feast that they are to feed upon is spiritual. Now, when we speak about a person being spiritual, we mean that that person is one who has been visited by the Spirit of God, and who has been visited by the Spirit of God specifically with respect to the matter of salvation: by faith ye are saved—it is not of yourselves, it is the gift of God. So that all who come to this table have that faith which is the gift of God wrought in their hearts, through the Word of God, by the Spirit of God.

These are the people who are invited to come to this table. They are spiritual, they are spiritually minded, and they understand spiritual things. The man who is not spiritual, the man who is carnal, the man who is natural, he understandeth not the things of the Spirit of God. There is nothing for him at this table here but to be eating and drinking damnation to himself. But those who are spiritual, those who are looking to Christ, those who are dependent upon Christ, they are invited to this table.

Now, because the grace of faith is in the heart, it is something that people do not see. But because this table is visible, everyone inside these four walls will see the bread broken and the wine poured out, and they'll see the people of God partaking of that bread and wine. Spiritually, in their hearts, they will be feeding upon Christ, but sitting at the table and partaking is visible. Therefore, those who come to this table not only have a spiritual life in their hearts, but they behave in a visible way outwardly, so that the officers of the church, the minister and the elders, in the kirk session, are able to judge, as far as they can, the spiritual condition of those who come forward. That is what the fencing of the table means. Those who come to this table, the spiritual people who come to this table, are told to examine themselves. This public fencing of the table describes on the one hand those who have a right to come, and invites them to come, and on the other hand it debars those who have no right to come. This is a public exercise of self-examination, and it takes to do with what is evident.

Therefore we debar from this table all those who do not have a delight in prayer. Those who are not praying people are not to come to the Lord's Table. We debar those who do not live in the atmosphere of prayer. The Lord's people are not merely sometimes in prayer, but prayer is their element—they're praying going along the street, they're praying in their beds. They're moving in an atmosphere of prayer, because they are poor and needy, and therefore prayer is something that they delight in. Now, in saying that, I'm not saying that they always have delight in their own prayers, or even that they have delight in praying, but nevertheless, there are times when the Spirit of grace and supplications assists them, as it is promised. We know not what to pray for as we ought, but the Spirit maketh intercession in our souls with groanings which cannot be uttered (Romans 8:26). The Lord's people are often ashamed of their prayers, but the fact is that it is a mark of a spiritual man and a spiritual woman that they are praying. They are praying in secret. They are also looking for an answer to their prayers, praying and looking upward to expect an answer to their prayer.

Now we debar from the table all who are heads of households and who do not keep family worship in the home. Any father who is spiritually minded has a concern for the souls for his children, and not only for himself, and he often pleads for them—of course he does—and prays for them. If he does do so, then he will have family worship in his home, and his children will be there to worship with him and to learn that the parents have a regard for God and a regard for God's worship. Now we debar all those who are heads of households—let me repeat, all those who are heads of households—who do not keep family worship. I know of cases of young people who would like to have family worship in their home, and their father is so brutish that he will not have it. Now I'm not referring to you if that's your situation—don't let Satan be tempting you on that point—I am referring to the heads of households who do not have family worship in their homes. But if that is true of anyone here this day, then I exhort you that from this very day you begin to have family worship in your home.

Now we debar from the Lord's Table all those who have no delight in the house of prayer. 'My Father's house', said the Lord, 'shall be called the house of prayer.' And if you pray in secret then you will rejoice in the house of prayer, because God gives a promise that he will make his people joyful in the house of prayer (Isaiah 56:7). What an astonishing thing this is to the people of this world, to those who find their joys in the football match, in the television, and so on! What an extraordinary thing it seems! It is another world to them—of course it is—to think that God is promising to make souls joyful in the house of prayer. But it is so because prayer is part of fellowship with God, and prayer is part of the public worship of God. Therefore those who despise the house of prayer, who are not attentive to the means of grace on Sabbath and on weekday, are debarred from this table. If that is the case with you, there is no clearer evidence that you are not spiritual. It means in fact that you cannot say with the spiritually minded people of God, 'How lovely is thy dwelling place, / O Lord of hosts, to me! / The tabernacles of thy grace / how pleasant, Lord, they be!' (Psalm 84:1). Can you say that? Can you really? Can you really say that when you come to the house of God you find it a pleasant experience? Or is it the fact that you don't find it a pleasant experience and therefore you don't come regularly? Well, you are debarred from this table until a change comes over you.

We debar from this table those who break the commandment that God has given to preserve the Sabbath day, to keep it holy. This is the day when we are to engage in the public and private worship of God in a particular way, and not only because of God's command but because it is an emblem of heaven, as those who are spiritually minded know from the Word of God. Heaven is a rest. 'They rest from their labours' (Revelation 14:13). It is a *sabbatismos*, a rest, the keeping of a Sabbath. Heaven is an eternal Sabbath, and those who cannot keep the Sabbath in time, whatever the reason is, are not going to enjoy the Sabbath of eternity. Some people try to explain that it's a Jewish ordinance and so on, but we know from the Word of God that heaven is an eternal Sabbath. The Lord's people call the Sabbath a delight, and honourable, and those who do not keep the Sabbath—those who engage in works which are not works of necessity and mercy—they are debarred from this table. They do not regard the Sabbath as a delight, neither are they obedient to God's commandment. It is most important that we take a firm grasp of that nowadays, when every effort is being made by governments and public institutions and employers to cause people to break the Sabbath. There is a full-scale attack being made on the Sabbath, and therefore it is an essential part of the witness of the Lord's people that they remember the Sabbath day to keep it holy. Those who break this day are debarred from this table, as they give evidence that they are not spiritually minded, and that they are not on their way to the *sabbatismos*, to the rest that remaineth for the people of God.

We debar from this table children who are disobedient to their parents. Now, in former years there were schoolteachers and others who spent a great deal of time telling the children, 'Your parents might be Christians but don't bother about their advice. Just do what we're telling you, because we're teaching you to learn things yourselves and to be independent,' and so on. Now they are discovering of course that that is resulting in things like vandalism and teachers being attacked and so on, and so suddenly they take a great leap and they begin to say that parents should be disciplining their children and they invent new codes of conduct. But you see the fact is that the obedience of children to their parents is not just a good social institution, it is a divine command. In fact it is a divine command so precious to God that it is the only commandment to which he has added a promise—the promise of long life, as long as that is consistent with the glory of God and the good of the Christian. So all children who are disobedient to their parents when they require them to do that which is lawful, they are debarred from this table.

And those who have the spirit of murder are debarred from this table: those who hate their brethren without a cause, who have that spirit in their hearts. Now as far as the Lord's people are concerned, their attitude to their fellows is summed up in three ways, or three exercises of love. First of all they have love to their own family, which is natural love, and secondly they have love to the people of God, which is spiritual love, and thirdly they have the love of compassion to the Christless, those who ready to perish. Now that is the view and the spirit of the people of God. Those who have a spirit of hatred are debarred from this table, because that is not the spirit of Christ.

We debar from this table all those who are guilty of sins against the seventh commandment. Sins against this commandment are so numerous in our day and generation and just appalling beyond description, but whatever may be true in other churches, we debar from this table all who are guilty and impenitent fornicators, adulterers, and sodomites both male and female. The very idea that practising that kind of sin is consistent with a Christian profession is abhorrent, and is contrary to the Word of God. Corinth was notorious for its immorality and its sodomy. But we know from the Word of God that some of those there who were guilty of that sin got repentance. They were justified in the Lord Jesus, they were washed from their sins. Instead of people accommodating to sodomy, sodomites should be told that they need repentance. Except they repent, they shall all likewise perish, and we say this out of concern for souls. We debar all such from the table.

Finally we debar from the table all those who are not upright in their life and conduct in the world. The people of God should be people of integrity. 'Thou shalt not steal.' Dishonesty, lying, covetousness—these sins are all descriptive of the carnal mind which is enmity against God and not subject to the law of God and neither indeed can be.

Now, on the other hand, we invite to this table those who are spiritually minded—those who have discovered what Paul discovered when he became spiritually minded: 'I am carnal,' he said. That is to say, we invite to the table those who know about the conflict between the spiritual mind and the carnal mind in their own souls, the spirit lusting against the flesh and the flesh against the spirit. This conflict weakens the child of God, especially in view of duties, but we invite to the table all of you who can really say, 'O wretched man that I am! who can deliver me from the body of this death?' (Romans 7:24).

We invite you to the table who know a difference between the Word of God being opened up to your soul and the Word of God being closed to your soul. There are times, whether in private or in public, when the Word of God is opened up to your soul, and you know the difference between that and the Word of God being closed to your soul. We invite you to the Lord's table, you of whom that is true.

We invite you to the Lord's Table if you know what it is to find the Lord. There are times when the soul can say they sought the Lord and they found him, and there are other times when the soul has to say, 'I sought him, but I found him not' (Song 3:1). We invite you to the table if you know the difference between finding the Lord and not finding him. And when you don't find him, how are you now when you don't find him? Well, then you are one with Mary Magdalene, who was weeping tears and saying, 'They have taken away my Lord, and I know not where they have laid him' (John 20:13). You are invited to come to this table in the hope that you will find the Lord there.

You are invited to come to this table if the cause of Christ is precious to you because Christ is precious to you. If Christ is precious to you, then all that belongs to him is precious to you, and you desire the wellbeing of Zion, that 'Sion by the mighty Lord / built up again shall be' (Psalm 102:16).

You are invited to this table who can say, 'The Lord's my strength and shield; my heart / upon him did rely' (Psalm 28:7). And what happened then? 'I am helped.' Very well, rely on him now and come to the Lord's Table and get help. You are invited to come, you of whom that is true.

You are invited to come if you have a place in your heart for the people of God, if there is a place in your soul that belongs to the people of God. You feel a drawing to them when you see them—even when you see them coming into church—you feel a drawing to them and you are glad that they're there in the worship. Now all those of whom this is true have passed from death to life, and therefore if this describes you, you are invited to come to the Lord's Table.

Lastly, you are invited to come to this table, you of whom it is true that this command of the Saviour, 'This do in remembrance of me,' has become a constraining command. Maybe there was a time when you resisted this command, you felt you were unworthy—but now this command has come to have a constraining effect on you. 'This do in remembrance of me.' You are coming to do this to acknowledge in the language of the Church that Christ is your beloved and your friend. Therefore you are invited to come.

Now we'll read those portions in the Word of God that distinguish this difference better than we can, firstly in Matthew chapter 5 and verse 2.

'And he opened his mouth, and taught them, saying, Blessed are the poor in spirit: for theirs is the kingdom of heaven. Blessed are they that mourn: for they shall be comforted. Blessed are the meek: for they shall inherit the earth. Blessed are they which do hunger and thirst after righteousness: for they shall be filled. Blessed are the merciful: for they shall obtain mercy. Blessed are the pure in heart: for they shall see God. Blessed are the peacemakers: for they shall be called the children of God. Blessed are they which are persecuted for righteousness' sake: for theirs is the kingdom of heaven. Blessed are ye, when men shall revile you, and persecute you, and shall say all manner of evil against you falsely, for my sake. Rejoice, and be exceeding glad: for great is your reward in heaven: for so persecuted they the prophets which were before you.'

And again in the epistle of Paul to the Galatians chapter 5 and verse 19.

'Now the works of the flesh are manifest, which are these; adultery, fornication, uncleanness, lasciviousness, idolatry, witchcraft, hatred, variance, emulations, wrath, strife, seditions, heresies, envyings, murders, drunkenness, revellings, and such like: of the which I tell you before, as I have also told you in time past, that they which do such things shall not inherit the kingdom of God. But the fruit of the Spirit is love, joy, peace, longsuffering, gentleness, goodness, faith, meekness, temperance: against such there is no law. And they that are Christ's have crucified the flesh with the affections and lusts. If we live in the Spirit, let us also walk in the Spirit. Let us not be desirous of vain glory, provoking one another, envying one another.'

And may the Lord bless the reading of these portions of his Word.

12 Come unto me

MATTHEW 11:28-30
Come unto me, all ye that labour and are heavy laden, and I
will give you rest. Take my yoke upon you, and learn of me;
for I am meek and lowly in heart: and ye shall find rest unto
your souls. For my yoke is easy, and my burden is light.
LORD'S DAY MORNING, INVERNESS, 22ND NOVEMBER 2009

Now we notice from the preceding verses that the Saviour is praising
God the Father for his sovereignty: 'I thank thee, O Father, Lord
of heaven and earth, because thou hast hid these things from the wise and
prudent, and hast revealed them unto babes.' But the fact that he praised his
Father and acknowledged the sovereignty of his Father did not prevent him
issuing this invitation to all to whom the gospel comes, the gospel in which
he sets forth that salvation in which his glory is declared to be very great.

1. The invitation
2. We are invited to come to Christ
3. The two kinds of rest which Christ promises

1. The invitation
They are labouring. They are labouring because they are in the yoke of sin.
'Whosoever committeth sin', says the Saviour, 'is the servant of sin' (John

8:34). Those who are referred to here as labouring are those who are being led and guided by sin.

The yoke of sin is something internal. God says that sin reigns in the human soul unto death. The yoke of sin is powerful because it is in the reigning faculty of the soul. Now the reigning faculty of the soul is its will. It is by the will that the soul *determines* what it will do, and by its will it *does* the things that it does. Now, as we are by nature, sin is reigning in the will, and therefore the soul is in bondage. The soul is in the yoke of sin, and led by the power of sin.

That is labour. People are labouring in the service of sin in the hope of obtaining happiness and peace. But because sin is reigning in them, what they are really seeking after and obtaining is instead the lust of the eye and the lust of the flesh and the pride of life, the very things which have characterised sinners since the first sin of Eve in the garden of Eden. Where sin is reigning, the sinner is labouring after happiness and peace of mind. But because he is under the yoke of sin, he never attains what he wishes and what he longs for. He eventually discovers more and more that this is a labour, and it's a labour which he cannot deliver himself out of.

As they are labouring in the yoke of sin, they are the servants of sin, and consequently there must be the wages of sin. We are told in the Word of God that the wages of sin is death (Romans 6:23). As they labour, endeavouring in one form of pleasure and another to find some rest and peace for their minds and souls and lives, so they add sin to sin, adding the burden of the guilt of all their sins to themselves. As they labour in striving after rest through the service of sin, they find out more and more that it cannot be. So by being in the yoke of sin and following sin and adding sin to sin, they are treasuring up wrath against the day of wrath. The burden which lies on them is the burden of the guilt of sin, and where the guilt of sin is, the soul is exposed to the wrath and curse of God, both in time and in eternity.

2. We are invited to come to Christ

This is an invitation to find rest. It is, in fact, an invitation to find rest in Christ. This is the real place to find rest. As you may remember, this is what

Augustine was expressing to God in his well known words, 'Thou hast made us for thyself, and we are restless till we rest in thee.' God made us for himself and we are restless until we rest in God.

The person who is giving the invitation says, 'Come unto *me*.' In order for us to enjoy the promise contained in the invitation, we must *come to him*. It is very important for us to have a clear understanding of this—that the promise which is made to those who labour and heavy laden is only fulfilled in the case of those who are labouring and heavy laden *and who come to Christ*. All the promises of God are really to graces of the Spirit in the soul (as you see here, the grace of faith), and there is no finding of the rest that is referred to here apart from coming to the one who is giving the invitation.

As he refers to himself in this chapter, he is, in his own person, the Son of God—the co-equal of the Father and the Holy Ghost, the same in substance, equal in power and glory with the Father and the Holy Ghost. He is very God of very God, the brightness of the Father's glory and the express image of his person.

But here he is giving this invitation not only as the Son of God, but also as the appointed Mediator between God and man. His very appointment signifies that God is willing to be reconciled to sinners through this Mediator—that God is willing to be reconciled to rebellious sinners, to hell-deserving sinners, to guilty sinners. Christ would never have given this invitation if he had not been appointed to be the Mediator between heaven and earth, between God and guilty man. But because he was indeed appointed to be the Mediator, he does give this invitation. It's part of what he is engaged to do—to reconcile sinners to his Father, and in so doing, to give them rest. Augustine was right to say we are restless until we rest in him, for in all the attractions of the world—attractions of every description and kind—the soul of man can find no true rest, as they learn by bitter experience.

At the same time, Christ promises rest not only because of who he is, but because of what he has done. As the Mediator between God and man, he has brought about reconciliation between God and man. He undertook to carry the guilt of the sins of a number that no man can number in his own body on the tree of Calvary. There was no rest for him until he drank the cup that was filled with the wrath and displeasure and curse of God against the sins of those for whom he died. 'The cup which my Father hath given me, shall I not drink it?' (John 18:11). Drink it he did! He drank it to the very dregs, until the cup was empty as far as the curse was concerned.

3. The two kinds of rest which Christ promises

It is because of this fact—his finished work on Calvary—that he is in a position to give rest.

First of all Christ gives deliverance to a sinner labouring in the yoke of sin by breaking that *power* of sin. Christ is able to cause that sin will no longer have dominion over the sinner. It is the Holy Spirit who enters the soul and who breaks the reign of sin and fulfils the promise that sin shall have no more dominion over you (Romans 6:9). The Saviour is able to promise this freedom from the rule of sin because he has received the Holy Spirit without measure. So when he does send his Spirit in this way, one form of rest which the sinner is granted is freedom from being wearied by going after the false promises which sin makes.

Secondly, he also gives rest with regard to the burden of *guilt*. The Saviour has willingly and lovingly died, and in his death he has provided shed blood which has the efficacy to cleanse from all sin (1 John 1:7). So in this rest there is not only the breaking of the power and reign of sin, but there is also the pardon of iniquity. As the Word of God says, 'where sin hath reigned unto death, grace reigns through righteousness unto eternal life by Jesus Christ our Lord' (Romans 5:21). Grace reigns to life and to rest and to peace, so that the sinner who is thus invited to this rest is promised deliverance both from the labour and from the burden of sin.

Now the point that I mentioned already, I need to stress again. The invitation is given openly, freely, to all to whom the gospel comes, but the promise that is in the invitation only applies to those who come. 'Come unto me,' the Saviour says. It is those who come to him—those who realise their need of deliverance and realise the value of the invitation and those who obey the invitation—who are the ones who inherit the rest that is promised. 'Come unto me, and ye shall find rest unto your souls.' Instead of being under the yoke of sin, they shall taste of the freedom and pardon of sin and the breaking of the power of sin in their spiritual experience—but they must *come to the Saviour*.

We must never lose sight of this fact, that it's those who obey the invitation who enjoy the blessing. Therefore it will not do for you and me to simply say, 'Well, the Saviour is inviting us.' We'll never get the rest until we *come to the Saviour*, until we believe in the Lord Jesus Christ—until we trust him as the alone Saviour provided by God the Father—until we come to him as the one who is saying, 'Come unto me, all ye that labour and are heavy laden, and I will give you rest.'

Now we would like to go on to mention the exhortation that he gives. Christ delivers from the yoke of sin, but here he speaks of another yoke. 'Take my yoke upon you, and learn of me.' The soul that is delivered from the yoke of sin now comes to be in the same yoke as Christ. That is to say, as they served sin in the yoke of sin, now they come to serve Christ in the yoke of Christ. That's what he says: 'Take my yoke upon you and learn of me; for I am meek and lowly in heart.'

Now they are to find rest in fellowship with Christ—rest in obedience to Christ—rest of soul in delighting in Christ. Now, perhaps you are here and you may say, 'Well, someone like Martha did not find the yoke of Christ very easy—she was troubled over many things.' And that was true. But Martha missed out something with regard to the yoke, and therefore the Saviour pointed her to Mary, who was sitting at his feet and drinking in the words of eternal life. Those who come to have the yoke of Christ first of all learn the need of grace—the need of strength to serve the Saviour in a way that will be profitable to themselves and glorifying to the Saviour himself. So this is a different form of rest—it is the rest of pleasure, the rest of delight in serving Christ in our day and in our generation (as David did—he served Christ in his generation by the will of God).

So the Saviour says here not only that he will deliver them from the yoke of sin, but also that he wishes them to come under yoke to himself, to learn of him, to be led and guided by him, and to enjoy his fellowship—to walk in the light as he is in the light, and to have fellowship with him and with his people. This is the yoke of Christ, and it is eternally preferable to being under the yoke of sin. This yoke affords real happiness, real joy to the soul, not a happiness that disappears because it is false—the false happiness of the yoke of sin.

Well, the yoke of Christ brings happiness in a measure in time, but in eternity, there are pleasures for evermore (Psalm 16:11). Pleasures for evermore! His servants shall serve him, and even in eternal glory they shall delight in enjoying the fellowship of the one who says, 'Take my yoke upon you, for I am meek and lowly of heart, and ye shall find rest unto your souls. For my yoke is easy and my burden is light.'

But my strength is going, so let us conclude with prayer.

Eternal and ever blessed one, grant to bless thy Word to us. Give us light upon thy truth that the service of sin is a service that is a labour that is sad, a labour indeed that does never know rest at the end of it, for there is no rest, saith my God, to the wicked. We pray thee that thou wouldst bless thy Word to us on this occasion, that thou wouldst bring souls to see their need of finding Christ and coming under the yoke of Christ, and enjoying the rest that is to be found in the Saviour, from being under the yoke of sin and the burden of guilt. Bless each of us with thy favour which is better than life, and pardon our many sins. For Christ's sake. Amen.

Concluding Psalm

Psalm 107:26-31

They mount to heaven, then to the depths
they do go down again;
Their soul doth melt and faint away
with trouble and with pain.

They reel and stagger like one drunk,
at their wit's end they be:
Then they to God in trouble cry,
who them from straits doth free.

The storm is changed into a calm
at his command and will;
So that the waves which raged before
now quiet are and still.

Then are they glad because at rest
and quiet now they be:
So to the haven he them brings
which they desired to see.

O that men to the Lord would give
praise for his goodness then.
And for his works of wonder done
unto the sons of men!